FROM THE HEART

Rachel Tobin-Smith, MSW, LCSW
Dave R. Johnson, DNS, APRN, BC, LMFT, LCSW

Editor & Page Layout
Stephanie Jentgen

Cover Design
Joseph Jentgen, Advangelism Design

COVER PHOTOGRAPH

Photo of Nora Neiger, taken during the summer of 1962 in Kingsville, Ohio at her Grandpa Glenn's.

"My parents taught me that their gift of love would be forever and that passing on that gift to my children would be the best reward I could receive. Thank you for being the best parents ever. I love you. "

Nora Neiger

For information on bulk purchases or group discounts for this, please contact SCAN, Inc. at 800-752-7116 or 260-421-5002.

ACKNOWLEDGEMENTS

Since 1974, many faces have crossed our path. Faces like the three-year-old with bifocals. The 20-year-old mother who arrives at SCAN two hours early to make sure she doesn't miss her visit with her baby... The limping, silver-haired grandmother carrying a toddler, coming to SCAN to visit with another grandchild... The foster mom with four preschoolers in tow, each clutching one of her fingers as they cross the parking lot... The father crossing the street in the rain, a teddy bear tucked under his arm, to see his son... The social workers who zip up their coats on a freezing winter day and sling bags full of resource materials and diapers over their backs... Board members circling the parking lot looking for a space as they prepare to spend another lunch hour volunteering for a meeting... The hundreds of people who give their time to SCAN to help make a difference in the life of a child. All of these, and many more, make up the faces of SCAN.

As with our daily work, this book would not have been possible without the contributions of our friends. We wish to extend our heartfelt thanks to these new faces of SCAN that have made this project possible: donors, story contributors to this book, HealthCares Magazine/Providence Communications, LLC, and all the parents and families who have turned to SCAN to help them make lifelong memories.

Without them, this journey **"FROM THE HEART"** would not be possible.

TABLE OF CONTENTS

CHAPTER 4 - DADS

CHAPTER 5 - LIFE'S LESSONS

CHAPTER 6 -- WHEN ALL IS SAID AND DONE

PREFACE

Parenting is an arduous task... a joy... a trial... a journey. No relationship in our lives plays as lasting and significant a role as the one we have with our parents. Not long after you get to know a new acquaintance or friend, one often ends up talking about childhood, parents, or childhood memories. Our parents' influence permeates our lives no matter how old we are. Whether we are five and letting go of mom's hand to walk into kindergarten the first time, or fifty-five and letting go of our dying parent's hand, memories write themselves on our minds, waiting for stories to be told.

Our parents are the first to introduce us to love and security. They provide our most basic needs. Through our parents we learn to smile, trust, seek new ventures, and sometimes wander beyond the boundaries of permissibility, knowing that unconditional love waits for our return. We experience structure, rules, and discipline for the first time with our parents. They are the ones who teach us that babies are fed every two hours, nap time occurs every four hours, homework must be done after dinner, and we cannot eat dessert without first having eaten our vegetables. These lessons often shape who we are today. How often have you heard, "The apple doesn't fall too far from the tree" or "You sound just like your mother (or father)!" Sayings such as these serve as gentle reminders that traditions, attitudes and parenting styles flow from one generation to the next.

The memories and lessons we learn from our parents, and from being a parent, often are some of life's most significant. In celebration of SCAN's 30th anniversary, this book features passages from several individuals who are friends of SCAN and took time to reflect. Each story, memory or poem captures one aspect of parenting and helps make visible the often intangible aspects of this most important life role. By sharing our stories we reveal to each other the richness of our experience. When we share, we experience the tasting of life twice, first in the moment and then in the reflection. The sharing of stories from one generation to the next gives us time to recollect that which has been important to us along the way.

Although each parenting story appears unique in the moment, it is in our reflection that we more fully recognize the universal truths about parenting:

- Parents teach children and children teach parents.
- Favorite memories often have little lessons and big truths.
- Moms and Dads provide different roles.
- Life's lessons often are just a story away.
- Parents aren't born, they're grown.

We thank the many contributors to **"FROM THE HEART."** Their stories tell a vibrant tale of the demanding, yet rewarding, journey called parenting. It's a perfect way to remember why, for more than 30 years, SCAN has worked so hard to help parents in our community pass on good memories to their children.

Introduction

About one year prior to SCAN's 30th anniversary, a group of people were discussing how to celebrate such a momentous occasion. The usual ideas came up – having a party, creating a special sticker to go on all mail, sending out news releases announcing all that the organization had achieved for the families of northeast Indiana. But everyone wanted to recognize the hard work that the staff, volunteers, funders, and clients had accomplished for three decades with something truly special. It was felt strongly that whatever was created needed to have a positive theme about parenting and families as that was the goal SCAN has for all of its clients.

That's how this book came about.

"From The Heart" features true stories from SCAN staff, friends, and volunteers. Each narrative describes some part of the author's life that involves family. Grouped into five chapters, these stories contain moments humorous, sad, touching and happy. In addition to individual stories, each chapter is introduced by Rachel Tobin-Smith, MSW, LCSW and executive director of SCAN, and Dave Johnson, DNS, APRN BC, LCSW, LMFT and a professor of nursing from the University of Saint Francis. Just as important as the numerous degrees these two people have earned, is their own experience as parents, children, and family members.

If you're reading this book, it's likely that you enjoy stories about children, family and parenting. You may even be a friend of SCAN. Either way, thank you for your interest. We hope this book touches you the way it touched everyone at SCAN.

CHAPTER 1

CHILDREN TEACHING PARENTS

"The child is father of the man."
William Wordsworth

Few would deny that we learn much about life from
children. They are so honest and open. Their questions and
curiosity help us gain delight in the simple things in life that
we lose sight of as adults. When a child is hurt, or when they
naively point out they need us, or when they curl up in your
lap for no reason at all, they teach us what the real priorities of
life are.

From the time a child is born they begin to cue us as
to how to parent. Sometimes we realize it and sometimes we
do not. They tell us how hot to make the formula by their
unwillingness to drink it. They inform us when they are too
long past their nap or bedtime by becoming unbearable. They
let us know when we are doing a good job by smiling and
cooing. As they get older they still teach us how to parent.
The first grader who after the first week of school gets out
of the car quickly so no one can see mom kiss him good bye
is teaching mom it is time to let go. The 5th grader who sits
down next to you on the couch to watch a movie lets us know
that as a parent he still needs us. As teenagers, they clamor
for independence. They force us through their "adolescent

tantrums" to evaluate what are appropriate boundaries of curfews, activities, and friends.

We become better parents because of what our children teach us. We tend to say they are telling us what their needs are but in actuality they are molding us into fully functioning parents with the challenges they provide. Inside this chapter are a few stories from people who have learned from their children.

Thoughts from Rachel

My daughters are two years apart in age almost to the date. When they were ages two and four, I often dressed them alike. I combed their hair alike. And they had the same routines or schedules. One day we were going to a reception for a friend who was receiving an award. I did not have child care that day. I decided I would just dress the girls up and take them with me, as we only would stay long enough to offer my friend congratulations.

Each girl wore their pink dress, white tights, and black patent leather shoes. I combed Addie's hair and pulled it back and put a pink ribbon in it. I combed Gabriel's hair, pulled it back and was about to put a pink ribbon in it when she got up and ran and got a hair clip. She also undid her hair and put the clip in crooked on the side of her head. I was upset. We were going to an adult world and I wanted the girls to look adorable. I scolded her and fussed at her for ten minutes. She just wouldn't let me near her hair. She finally started to cry from me scolding her. She sobbed. Her sobbing stopped me cold. I asked myself, "How important is this hair ribbon and this hair style that I would bring my child to tears over it?" Of course in my head I realized it was not important at all. It was such an important lesson in parenting that Gabriel taught me that day. She taught me to pick my battles. She taught me that being in control, and having it my way was important to me, but what was important in raising a child was letting them have some control wherever you can. Letting children learn to make decisions builds self-esteem and life skills.

Reflections from Dave

Justin taught me to appreciate every moment. He was near his fifth birthday when we said our earthly goodbyes and I remember thinking I would never love anyone or anything again. I cried in the privacy of my shower and yelled at our world on my daily runs through Foster Park. Justin is the first-born son of my wife, Rosie, and me.

You notice that I still speak of Justin in the present. He'd be nearly 25 years old today, but he continues to teach me if I take the time to listen. The whispers of truth can be heard in the pauses of silence. I hear… "Touch, laugh, sweat, connect, play, kiss, enjoy, teach, pray, be strong, show faith, be kind, set boundaries, be firm, be soft, and be present!" Call it what you will, but in our world of multi-tasking I sometimes become a bit distracted from some of my life's priorities. Justin sometimes screams for me to be present when I am being distracted. Whether the call comes at 11pm from a college daughter or the plea from my 7th grade son who needs help with a project, I hope to be present. I recently captured the "present" as I danced the daughter-daddy dance at my oldest daughter's wedding. "The present" was pure joy and fun of "being" with my wife and children. We created memories that we will cherish the rest of our lives.

All too often my body is one place and my mind is in another. I always want to listen and learn from my children. They have much to teach.

THE OTHER SIDE

Lynn M. Noneman

The best advice I can give a parent is simple. Hang In There.

Those three words may sound too simple, but trust me, they are not. Through the tumultuous middle-school years, the trying teenage years, the worrisome college years – just hang in there.

Someone whom I admire and respect once told me that parenting is the hardest job you will ever have. She was right, but it is also the most rewarding – once you make it to the other side. I have made it to the other side and it <u>was</u> all worth it, as you will see when you read the following letter. My daughter sent this letter to me when she was 25 years old. I asked her if it was okay with her if I could submit it for all the world to see. I didn't want to embarrass her or betray a confidence, but I was so proud of her and I wanted to share our story with everyone. She had no idea that this letter had meant so much to me until that moment. Thank you for letting me share it with you.

10-29-03

Dear Mom,

So, I'm sitting here thinking all these deep thoughts and I thought I ought to share them with you. Since most of them are about you anyway.

This week has been pretty tough. And it's only Wednesday. And it's been tough for everyone, not just me. But all that got me thinking about you.

Here I am in my own apartment, sharing my life (almost) with a wonderful man, and almost all grown up. And it all boils down to this... the fact of the matter is, I still need you! Yea, I'm doing okay on my own. But sometimes I still need my mommy!

Ever since I can remember, you've always been there for Cherise and me. When times got hard when dad left, you worked your butt off to provide for us. You made time to make us feel special by doing the big and the little things. Even taking time to put "I love you" notes in our lunches. And when you and Mark got married, you taught me one of many valuable lessons. I think the reason I disapproved of the two of you was not so much that I wanted you and dad to get back together, but that I thought you would stop loving me as much as you did. And that you would give that love to Mark. I was jealous of your love for him. It was <u>my</u> *love,* <u>my</u> *attention. And now he had it. But I was wrong. Very wrong.*

You loved me even more because you brought someone into our lives that truly cared for all of us. Mark loved us and provided for us. And it taught me that even though you were trying to better your life and make yourself happy, your thoughts were always of Cherise and me first. You knew what kind of a man Mark was. That he would love your children as his own (no matter how much of a pain we were sometimes.) You knew he was a good man and that's why you brought him into our lives. And mom, I thank you for that! Not just for marrying a wonderful man, but for putting us first, as well, like always.

(Now, I know you're getting misty. So dry your eyes so you can read the rest of my letter.)

But my point is, even as adults, the two of you have always been there for us. You know when to step aside and when to kick us in the behind (you should write a book or something.)

Even though I'm grown up and am trying very hard to be an independent adult, I want you to know that I still need you. I need you to pat me on the back, to listen when I need someone to talk to, to give me a shoulder to cry on, to harp on me when things need to get done (even though it's irritating as hell, I still need it.) But, most of all, I need you to be proud of me and not disappointed if I didn't turn out exactly the way you and Mark had planned. And to encourage my little goals as well as my big ones. The way you always have.

Mom, I love you so much! I admire you in more ways then you know. A wonderful husband, beautiful home, outstanding wife, a great and successful career, spectacular mother and two pretty darn great kids that Mark had more than a big hand in helping. These are just a few accomplishments that came to mind. Not to mention the best looking grandmother of two (as of yet) that I know. And sometimes I think you need to be reminded of that.

I wish for myself to even come close to the things you've accomplished. Cherise has already followed in your footsteps. I only have the opportunity. And I think and hope that I'm on the right path so far. I know that when the time comes, I'm going to be a great wife and a fabulous mother and with any luck and a prayer – a good art teacher. I know I will. I had a pretty good teacher myself. You!

Mom, thank you! Thank you for always giving 100% of

yourself. For always being there for us and opening your home and your heart to the ones we've brought along the way. Just know that I still need you. Every day! And not just as my mother, but as my friend, too. Thanks for being the wonderful you that you are.

I love you very much! Always! Your daughter,

Bugs

P.S. Don't worry. I'm not sick, pregnant or eloping. I just wanted you to know how much I appreciate all you've done.

**"All that I am or ever hope to be,
I owe to my angel Mother."**

Abraham Lincoln

JUMPING WAY PAST CONCLUSIONS

Jerri Lerch

I think that most children are very, very bright. With support, encouragement, and lots of stimulation in a wide variety of ways, they thrive. As responsible parents, we have felt it to be our duty to provide logical explanations to the multitude of questions that any child asked, being careful not to extend into more detail than our child was prepared to handle.

Our son, Ross, was precocious and articulate at an early age. When he was four-years-old, he could play Monopoly and make change for $1,000. We listened to the nightly news together as a family. We had two fish in the family aquarium that were named "Ronnie" and "Nancy". At five-years-old, he knew what the "White House" was and, much to our surprise, he asked for a George Bush button to wear to school during the presidential campaign. So it wasn't a complete surprise when during that timeframe, he asked me what the word "stock" meant.

I was somewhat amazed at how far his awareness of the world had expanded. I proceeded to talk with him about owning things. He owned his toys. As parents, we owned cars and our home. And, I told him that some things were too big to be owned by parents or any one person. I mentioned big companies, like McDonald's, that many people own together. Ross listened intently, his big brown eyes focusing on my face.

I explained that big companies were owned by lots and lots of people. When someone became an owner, they were given paper stock certificates representing how much of the company they owned. I looked at him, pausing a moment to assess his understanding and for him to ask any questions that he might have.

I'll never forget when he said, "OK, Mom, but what about 'Jack and the Bean <u>stalk</u>'?" I had assumed that I had understood him.

During that same time period, I made a similar error in listening and responding to an even bigger question. He asked me what "hell" meant. My mind immediately raced to all of the religious training that I'd had to draw upon for this moment. I did wonder where he might have heard the word and I didn't like the thoughts that were entering my head. After all, this child rode the public school bus to kindergarten and first grade every day.

I quickly began describing how some people believed in a beautiful place called "heaven" that was reserved for people who are good to other people. Then I tried to explain that some people also believed in an ugly, uncomfortable place called "hell" which is were people went who did lots of really bad things in their life.

Again, I looked at him intently to see if he understood. Again, I received the attentive, brown-eyed stare, absorbing every word. Again, I heard those famous words, "OK, Mom, but what about…?" followed by, "Hail, Hail, Aurora", in

<u>Sleeping Beauty</u>.

After many good laughs at my misunderstandings, I finally learned my lesson. I never again offered an explanation without first making sure I really understood what my son was asking of me.

"A child can ask questions that
a wise man cannot answer."

Author Unknown

ARE YOU CRYING?

Cherise A. Copeland

When raising a two-year old and a two-month old, things become very busy and rather hectic. But every once in a while there is a moment that helps you slow down and laugh.

My daughter, Isabelle, has been adjusting to having a new little brother. She is wonderful with him and so very caring. Any time he makes the slightest little noise, she says, "Mommy, Dylan is cryin'."

I explained to her that he doesn't always cry, sometimes he is just fussy. Then, the next time her little brother starts making noise, she would let me know again that he is crying.

One morning, I took Isabelle to the park. She was having a blast running around and playing on the equipment. She got a little careless, lost her footing and fell. Of course I saw the whole thing and could do nothing but run to her after she hit the ground. I immediately cradled her, checking for any scratches, blood, or broken bones. She cried for a bit, which seemed more of a whimper. She was fine, just a bit shaken up. After wiping away the tears and dirt, she got right back out there and started playing again. I was so proud of her, and myself. I kept it together. I was strong and calm.

We finished playing at the park and then loaded up in the car to go home. As I was driving home I kept replaying the image of my daughter falling from the playground equipment, and what could have happened. I started to cry. Isabelle heard me and asked if I was crying. She doesn't like it when I get upset so I told her no. She stopped and thought for a second and then asked, "Are you fussy?" This short little question made me laugh, and helped me appreciate the little things in my life.

"Children seldom misquote you. In fact, they usually repeat work for word what you shouldn't have said."

Unknown

CELEBRATE THE DIFFERENCES

Lorene R. Arnold RNC, MSN NP

Parenting brings out intense emotions. I sometimes look at my children and think my heart could break from loving them so much. But there also are times of frustration and anger when I wonder how I ever thought I could be a good parent. Then I go into their room when they have fallen asleep and look at those angelic faces, and think, "How could I have been so angry such a short time ago? They are beautiful little angels." This story deals with one of those times of frustration and anger, and what I learned from it.

It always amazes me how two children from the same parents can be so different in personalities, wants, and needs. This was made very clear to me one day when my daughter was about a year-and-a-half old, and my son was several months old. He was not sleeping through the night, and I was very sleep deprived. I began to wonder why I ever considered having two children so close together. Christopher was a very fussy baby compared to my daughter. When Jennifer was upset, I could cuddle, rock, or walk with her and she would settle down and fall asleep in my arms. When my son became upset, it seemed there was nothing I could do to help. He would just get more and more upset as I tried to comfort him.

On this particular day, he was crying and crying. I tried rocking him, walking with him, singing to him, and cuddling him, but the crying just continued. The longer it went on, the more frustrated we both became. It was a hot day, and we were both miserable. Finally, in a fit of frustration because he would not stop crying, I took him into his room and put him in his crib. I was so angry with him and with my inability to console him that I was really afraid of what I might do to him. I felt like shaking him to try to get him to stop. Inside, I knew this would not help, yet I just remember that feeling of total exhaustion and frustration. I knew I had to put some space between us, so I placed him in his crib and left the room.

I went to my bed to lie down and began crying over my inability to console my own son. I had thought I was ready for children. I was a 35-year-old nurse who had wanted children for years. I had read all types of books on parenting, yet I was unable to console my son. I was feeling very alone, frustrated, and angry at myself. And, I must admit, I was angry at my son, too. Why wouldn't he let me console him? The monitor was on in Chris' room, and I suddenly realized he had stopped crying. I heard coos coming from the monitor. I crept back into his room, and he was cooing to himself looking in the crib mirror. As I walked into his room, he looked up at me and smiled.

I learned an important lesson that day. Children are individuals and what works for one, does not always work for another. That day, I remember thinking of how I need to treat each child as the individual they are, and not assume the same parenting skills will work for each child. From that day on, when my son would begin getting upset, I would put him in his crib with some books or toys, and he was much happier than being cuddled by me. My daughter, on the other hand, preferred the cuddling. As they are growing into teenagers, I still try to remember that they are individuals, and should not be compared to each other. Each has their own set of skills and talents, and are beautiful for whom they are.

"Even children of the same mother look different."
Korean Proverb

"WOW" TIMES: LITTLE PIECES OF THE BIG PICTURE

Dave R. Johnson

Often, some of life's most important truths come to me from the mouths of my children. Having a large family, I am blessed with frequent opportunities to hear a child's perspective.

A few years back, my daughter, Molly, and my son, Paul, both "got their wheels." Molly was 15 years old and learning to drive; Paul was five years old and wanted the training wheels taken off his bike. Both these transitions presented challenges and rewards at the same time. Teaching a daughter to drive is a story in itself. I have found that there are some streets in Fort Wayne on which no 15-year-old ever should be allowed to operate a motor vehicle. State Boulevard is one of these. However, I digress – we'll save that for another time!

As for Paul, he badgered me relentlessly to fix up his bike. He wanted the training wheels removed, and my wife, Rosie, and I decided to give his bicycle a complete "tune-up" to transform it into a little boy's "ride". (You see, this bike had been passed down from his four older sisters, so it sported pink handle grips and a pink seat.) Rosie dropped the bicycle off at the bike shop and requested new handle grips. She also requested a new back tire to replace the balding, worn piece of rubber currently serving as a tire. I figured a couple days and a few bucks later that we'd all be on our way.

A few days later, I stopped by the shop to pick up the transformed bicycle. I pulled $20 out of my wallet, smiling kindly at the owner. The bike repair person, smiling just as nicely, presented me with a bill for $45. What you need to understand is that this bike was probably worth $10 at a garage sale, and that's being generous. I was not prepared for a $45 bill. In asking about the charges, I found it wasn't only the handle grips that had been replaced, but the entire handle bar assembly. In addition, my wife had asked to have a kick stand added. (I remain unconvinced that a dirt bike, which gets thrown to the ground in between rides, actually needs a kick stand.) As for the balding tire, the store owner thought it could make it through one more child in its current condition, so he replaced the inner tube only. He beamed proudly at the thought that he had saved me some money.

Needless to say, all the way home I dwelled on the fact that I had just dumped $45 into a $10 bike. I arrived home for Paul's first riding lesson in less than the best of moods. "Forty-five dollars… can you believe it?" I announced as I came through the door. "Forty-five dollars for a 10-dollar bike. I could have bought half a new one for that!" Rosie looked at me, rolled her eyes, and, in all her wisdom said, "Dave, lighten up. Paul is so excited. Just enjoy him… enjoy the moment."

So, I joined Paul outside. We began our two-wheeler lessons on the lawn so Paul could learn to fall on soft ground. He made several runs on the grass before we moved to the pavement. For the first couple times on the sidewalk, I ran beside him. Each time he was about to fall, I held his bike and helped him regain his balance. Within a few minutes, Paul was riding solo, his bright, blue eyes flashing and his hair flying in the wind. It was there, in that moment, that Paul experienced the magic all bike riders experience sooner or later – the moment when it all comes together, balance takes over and the ability to ride a bike is imprinted on the brain, never to be lost.

I experienced that moment with Paul. He included me in his moment as he looked over at me and said, not only with his mouth, but also with his eyes and his whole body, "WOW!"

It was a "WOW" experience for Paul. He grabbed the moment and immersed himself in it. Because he included me, I felt it, too. I thanked God that afternoon for the "WOW" I had just experienced.

Kids are good at that – grabbing hold of an opportunity, forgetting the distractions and living in the moment for all it's worth. That's how life is meant to be lived. Sure, we have to be realistic. We have to be adults and handle the details. But, there's a lot to be said for just enjoying the moment. Sometimes, enjoying the moment with my children is difficult for me. Traumas of the past, stressors of the present, and pressures of the future get in the way. It is hard to block out distractions and appreciate the moment. However, with gentle nudges from an insightful wife, and the enthusiasm and innocence of my children, I am learning. Life moves very quickly and I don't want to miss the "WOWs." For it is in the midst of these experiences that I know I am blessed.

"Children are the reward of life."
Congolese Proverb

EXPECT THE UNEXPECTED

Mindy J. Yoder, MSN, APRN, BC

As a parent you have to be on your toes and "expect the unexpected" at all times. I am a mother of three small children, ages 8, 6, and 1½ . I also am a Certified Family Nurse Practitioner who is a full-time faculty member, teaching primarily pediatrics courses. So, you would think I would be ready for any possible situation that availed itself to me as a parent, right? Wrong.

I was taken off guard one afternoon when I was seated at a college graduation ceremony. On this momentous occasion, my "baby" brother was graduating from college and moving on to law school. My son, who was then 3 years old, was seated beside me in the front row of a reverently quiet but jam-packed overflow room in an auditorium as graduates crossed the stage on the screen in front of us to receive their diplomas. The rest of the story has three important lessons:

#1: Three-year-olds have not learned the skill of whispering yet.

#2: Three-year-olds try to be 100% honest in everything they say (most of the time).

#3: Three-year-olds are moving through Freud's developmental stage entitled the "phallic" stage.

One would think with my training and education that I would be prepared for just about anything my three-year-old would say. Sadly, that wasn't the case.

After an hour or so of the ceremony had passed, my son became quite bored. He began exploring his anatomy with his hands, which is a fairly common phenomenon during the phallic stage. Within a few minutes of this activity, my son turned to me and said in a non-whispering voice, "Mommy, my p_ _ _ _ is growing long and hard". As giggles could be heard from rows around me, I was speechless as I sunk down into my chair. With 18 years of education plus 5 years of clinical experience in family practice, all I could think to do was lean down and whisper "that's nice honey, now remember we have to be real quiet and whisper…".

This story is one of my favorites for several reasons. First, the story demonstrates that each of us as parents will have moments where we do not have the textbook answer for dealing with our children. Second, no matter how much we think we know, parenting will always be a challenge. Finally, the story demonstrates Freud's phallic stage really well to my nursing students.

PRICELESS

Staci M. Kershner

My son, Devin, joined the Cub Scouts this year. For the final event of the year, they were able to go to the Wizards' baseball game and camp out on the infield. I'm not a very big fan of baseball or camping out. Needless to say, I was not excited about this event. We bought four tickets and took my nephew along with us.

For the first few innings of the game, my nephew couldn't understand why all these people were there in the stadium. He didn't realize that they were watching a baseball game. The boys were more fascinated watching the cotton candy guy walk up and down the aisle and every time he came closer to us, the boys would look at Kent and me and say, "PLEASE!!!" After about the sixth time of their wide-eyed pleading, we caved and bought them one cotton candy to share for $3.00! If you have ever read the book "If You Give a Mouse a Cookie" you know what happens next. They became thirsty! Two drinks and two ice creams cost another $17.00, as well as four trips to the bathroom to wash sticky hands, chocolate faces and take care of "business."

I was becoming frustrated, but told myself that things would be better once the game was over and they could run around on the field. I had no idea how many people actually participated in this camp out. However, we quickly found out. After the game ended, we hurried out to the car to retrieve our four sleeping bags, four bag chairs, four pillows, one cooler, one tent and a bag of snacks (we may as well have brought the kitchen sink, too!) The line to get back into the stadium curved from the first base gate to the main entrance. With gear in-hand, we shuffled through the line. Once in, we headed to the only open spot we could see... right beside home plate. We gave the boys two new baseballs and two pens and sent them with a friend to get autographs from the players. Kent and I set up camp. The boys ran and ran until about 2:30am. With Benadryl in hand, I said, "Boys, it's time for bed." Right before Devin closed his eyes he said, "Mom?" I snarled and barked "GO TO SLEEP!" He calmly said "I just wanted to tell you this was the BEST night of my life, thank you." I swallowed the lump in my throat and told him I loved him too, and he was welcomed.

And just like the MasterCard commercial....

New tent = $80.00

Four tickets to the baseball game = $55.00

Drinks and candy = $20.00

Hearing my son say it was the BEST night of his life = Priceless

LOOK FOR WHAT YOUR CHILDREN ARE DOING RIGHT

Adrienne M. Clark

"Strength based" is how we describe programs at SCAN. The message of looking for and focusing on strengths weaves itself throughout the instruction and training our home-visiting staff receives. As one of the program trainers, I have talked this talk for a long time. I have also learned to walk the walk. After all, how long can you say something without eventually listening to yourself and applying your own good advice?

Look for what your children are doing right... and tell them. I have found that one message to be so very powerful. It has changed my relationship with each one of my six adult children. When they were young, I often gave advice (usually unsolicited) and made sure the kids knew when I felt they needed to change their ways. Of course, this led to many arguments over the years, and things always seemed tense between me and one or the other of them. Of course, they seldom paid attention to what I said anyway.

Now, how things have changed! I find they are always happy to hear I am coming for a visit. (Most of them live far enough away for it to be a "trip" to go see them.) They will call and ask when I'm coming if they think too many months have gone by without a visit. And they call often asking for my advice. Well, maybe they're not as direct as that, but they call and discuss things with me in a way that lets me know they want to know what I think.

What brought about this miracle? I simply began focusing on their strengths and then commenting on them. I ignored all those little things that used to drive me crazy... usually things over which I had no control. The wonderful thing about focusing on the positive in each child is that once I started looking for them, I found more and more of those positives to acknowledge. It's great! The more wonderful things I see in my children, the more positive I feel about the job I did parenting them.

Everybody wins. We all feel wonderful about ourselves. As an added bonus, they are more open to input from me and offer me the opportunity to share my "wisdom" with them. They actually hear me... and we no longer have those tense times we once had.

DINNERTIME LESSONS

Janice Schenkel

Growing up in a large Catholic family – there were nine of us including our parents – the evening meal served as the gathering place for all to share their day's experiences. During the 1960s and early 1970s this was easy to do as there were no structured sporting events for girls, (I had four sisters), and the two brothers were just toddlers. We were lucky in that we did have one TV in the house. It was not allowed to be "on" during mealtime and, of course, there was no cable or computer to distract us. All of our friends were home eating with their parents. Dinner was a time for praying and sharing, always a fun place to be each evening.

Being the second oldest, I had to help with meal preparation and clean-up, which was the normal, expected thing to do. I married in 1974, and continued the Sunday meal tradition with my parents, my husband's parents and, over the years, our four children. Mealtime in our house remained as it was when we grew up. Prayers before meals, no TV, discussions of the days' events, politics, religion and sports took place.

During the 1990s, as our three sons reached their high school years, many of their friends would spend after school and evening hours at our place. We never objected, as these young boys were truly wonderful human beings. They just wanted some individual attention from a father figure and some love and guidance, which my husband gave them on a routine basis. Some of them had parents who worked all the time and others were from single-parent families. Many of these young men confided in my husband and me on a regular basis. Over the years, they gradually became a part of mealtime with us and assisted in meal preparations and clean-up.

There was one young man who, during his senior year of high school, began coming around with the others. Though he had grown up with dysfunctional parents, he was a great young man. He was amazed that we actually had food in our refrigerator and that it was shared with all the children that came to our home. He was here many evenings during mealtime but would not eat with us. He would inform us that he was not hungry and wanted to just watch TV during mealtime. We allowed him to do so in another room where it would not distract the rest of us, which usually numbered 8 to 12 people. I always left a plate of food for him to eat when we finished cleaning up the kitchen, and he would then eat alone, hours later, after everyone else was done.

Over the course of a few months he slowly would help with meal preparation and clean-up, but he never would eat with us. We would ask him every time, just once, and when he declined we would let him be. After about 5 months of this, some of the others finally talked him into eating with us. He did join us at the table and my husband and I were secretly thrilled that he wanted to become a part of our "family" time.

He did comment to me later that he said he did not feel
that he had anything to offer us in return for actually being
allowed to sit down and eat with us as family, as that was
something he had never done. I told him his presence was the
only gift he needed to give to us, as he was truly a lovely and
loving person. He joined us for many meals after that and we
enjoyed every minute of it. We soon learned he truly was a
conversationalist and we could talk with him for hours.

   As patience is not one of my strong virtues, I often look
back on this occasion as a reminder to me that this young man
taught me something far greater than I gave to him. He taught
that patience and trust are needed in any relationship for it
to grow and that one needs to develop that trust in his or her
own time frame. He needed his time to feel that he was loved
by those surrounding him and that we would not leave or
harm him in anyway.

   A few years ago, we attended a wedding. Four of
the young men and women who dined with us during their
teen years also were there. They are now dating, preparing
to marry or are married with children. They made it a point
to tell us that one of the most important experiences they
remember about their high schools years was the sharing of
meals with us. They truly appreciated our time together and
learned that a family that prays and dines together has many
great experiences to share. My husband and I (married almost
30 years now) were surprised and touched by their kind words
and their discussion of the happy experiences at our home. We

just assumed we were doing what everyone did as a family and were thankful for our health and happiness together. But these young people told us that we had played an important role in their lives, teaching them about the greatness of God and family. Each of them said they will always remember that with their new families.

One never really knows how important something as simple as a meal can be. We are truly grateful for our parents who showed us that guidance, love and just being there (along with some food) are the most important elements of a successful and happy life together.

PAUSE AND REFLECT

Take a moment and think about your own experiences as a child, parent, or grandparent.

1. What important lessons have your children taught you?

2. How will you continue to remember these lessons when you're distracted" by the day-to-day business of life?

3. How have your children transformed you into whom you are today?

4. What stories do you want to recall about these lessons?

CHAPTER 2

FAVORITE MEMORIES

*"Youth lives on hope,
old age on remembrance."*
French Proverb

Even though childhood only lasts the first 20 years
of your life, the memories created during that time live
on forever. These recollections are not always warm and
cheery. Some are sad, some hurt, and others make us laugh.
The memories of our parents and of growing up are the
background for most of our life, much like the musical score
of a movie. They play on and on. Different memories appear
just like a different piece of music plays as the scenes change in
our favorite film.

Creating "good" memories for our children is
important in our role as parents. Good memories can be
about lessons learned. They also can teach children how to
be effective parents in the future. These memories, without
a doubt, teach us to trust, to love, to have strength, and to
face life. Often the lessons learned, and recalling how we
learned them, become some of the most important scenes in
our lives, helping us to become fully-functioning adults. These
memories play through our mind like a melody, even when
we are not aware of it. This section features some of these

memories. Enjoy!

Thoughts From Rachel

My memories have become so important, now that both my parents are gone. I can remember vividly, after a long day at work, my dad taking the time to walk beside me as I rode my tricycle on the sidewalk in front of our house. I can hear my mother's words as clearly now as I could when I was young, telling me to "stop wiggling" and to "be a good soldier." I also can recall the strong bond between my parents as my mother and father would chatter for hours each evening about the day and life's events. I still can hear the raspy "I love you, too" my mother spoke to me two days before she died...

Reflections from Dave

Memory making is about retelling a story from the past. Often it starts in the whispers of bedtime when we snuggle our children with the lights out and reflect on day's end. It occurs at the supper table when we ask broad questions about "best parts" of vacations, holidays, and school days. Making memories occurs when we re-tell a story from our own childhood followed up with the "lessons" we learned. Just as we enjoy hearing a favorite musical piece over and over again, our children appreciate the old familiar stories. Often there are bits of wisdom in these stories, and lessons unfold as our children grow older and come to appreciate some of the inner workings of our words and pasts. In reflecting on "favorite" memories we choose to taste life again... first in the moment and then in the reflection.

MEMORABLE MOMENTS

Lynda L. Crawford

When my daughter, Ellen, was very young, we were shopping at Wal-Mart just before Memorial Day. She became really excited about something she obviously thought was wonderful and wanted to know if she could have money to buy it. I asked her what she wanted to purchase, and, after a bit of prompting, she told me that she had seen a beautiful bunch of flowers that had a sign on them that said "Mom". She wanted to buy them for me. I realized that what she had seen was a grave decoration. Now, when either of us sees memorial decorations, we recall her very sweet and innocent thought with a gentle laugh.

One January when my son, Robbie, was small, the city of Auburn was handing out seedling evergreen trees to plant when you brought your Christmas tree to their recycling facility. Robbie thought that was great, and he helped to plant our new tree with great care. A few days later, I looked outside and saw our side yard had become home to several used Christmas trees. About that time, I saw Robbie coming down the street dragging a tree that was about twice his size. He had gone around the neighborhood and collected discarded trees so that we could trade them in for more "new trees".

Steve was my first-born, and when he was small he stayed with my mom while I worked. Since my dad was retired and my grandmother lived with my parents,

Steve didn't want for much of anything; his wish was their command. For instance, cowboy boots and watches were a couple of his favorite items, so he always had boots and a "tick-tock". Daniel Boone was one of his favorite TV shows, and he was convinced he needed "a Daniel Boone hat". We all kept our eyes open for one of these special caps, but we weren't able to come up with anything. Then, out of nowhere, appeared this hat that Steve thought was absolutely the greatest thing since sliced bread. As it turned out, my mom had found a dead squirrel in the back yard (at least she said that was what happened — we can only hope!), and yes, she cut off the tail and made a hat for Steve.

THE LAKE COTTAGE

Paul Helmke

My favorite childhood memories generally have something to do with summers spent at my grandparents' lake cottage.

My brother, sister and I would spend much of the summer at the lake with my parents, grandparents, and numerous cousins, aunts, and uncles. As kids, our days were full of activities. We'd wake up early and begin the endless array of fun. We'd play shuffleboard, swim, ski (once enough of the neighbors were up for the day and we could run the boat), sail, hike, play games both inside and outside (Monopoly, cards, volleyball) with occasional breaks for breakfast, lunch, and dinner. We weren't supposed to get back in the water until we had rested for 30 minutes or so.

Even the food tasted better at the lake! The "Sweet Sue" corn and tomatoes in August were always the best, but I was happy just eating the mulberries off of our neighbor's tree.

Everyone on the beach seemed to be related in some way and you felt welcome anywhere.

When I would begin to tire out, I enjoyed just taking it easy and reading in the bunkhouse.

I've been going to the same part of the same lake area my whole life. When my parents tore down the old cottage a couple years ago, I was a little sad since that cottage had been one of the constants in my life for 50+ years. The new house has been nice though, since it still captures elements of the old cottage. I'm happy that my two daughters were able to experience many of the same things at the same place when they were growing up as I did. When my brother and sister and relatives come to Indiana to visit, we still get together at "our" beach at "our" lake.

"Sweet childish days, that were as long
As twenty days are now."
William Wordsworth

MY FAVORITE THINGS

Shafonda M. Lewis

As a young girl, my favorite time of day was the afternoon. Once I finished my homework, I was able to go to the best youth center on the south side of town – the Pontiac Youth Center. Pontiac Youth Center is still in existence and helping children throughout the community.

One of my best memories as a child occurred when we used to participate in fundraisers in the community. This gave me an opportunity to see that there are people in the world who are willing to give, and it wasn't about inner city youth needing money.

As a teenager, I learned that when someone is trying to tell you something right from wrong, that you should definitely take time to hear that person out. As an adult, I appreciate my grandmother's words of wisdom.

The top lessons I learned as a child were 1) to respect others and elders, 2) to believe in God, 3) to give to others and not expect anything in return.

As an adult, I have learned in order to earn respect, you must give respect. I learned to be careful who you select as friends and who you trust.

Looking back, I realize the incredible gifts that my grandmother gave to me and my siblings. Because of a family crisis, she took time out of her life to raise all of us and other relatives. My grandmother could have said no and we could have been separated. Instead, she raised me to become the woman I am today. I personally thank God for having my grandmother in my life.

My favorite relatives are my sisters. I'm glad that my grandmother raised us to stick together, respect each other, and be there for each other regardless of the situation. If I needed to call on any of my sisters, I know that they would be there to support me.

"Home – that blessed word, which opens to the human heart the most perfect glimpse of Heaven, and helps to carry it thither, as on angel's wings."
Lydia M. Child

CHILDHOOD MEMORIES

Mark E. Souder — Member of U. S. Congress

There was a special time of day with each of my
parents when I was growing up. When I arrived home from
school, often the first thing I did was fill my mom in on the
day's activities. Not surprisingly, being a Type A temperament
from the beginning, I would pace around our kitchen table,
munching on Seyfert's potato chips, unloading the day's events
to which my mom provided commentary, mostly sympathetic.
Most evenings my dad would spend time with me just before
I went to sleep, sometimes just a few minutes before he went
back down to the store to finish up the evening's work and
other times an hour or more discussing things of life. Both not
only provided guidance, but demonstrated their love by caring
and giving of their time.

Vacation time was always our family highlight. We
generally went for two weeks in the summer to northern
Michigan and southern Ontario. This was my dad's big
release from long work weeks at the furniture store. But it
wasn't just that we went on vacation. My father took movies
and slides of each trip. So we would gather as a family
multiple times in anticipation of vacation, eating popcorn and
preparing ourselves for the time away. Then upon return,
we would watch that year's pictures for a few months. One
slide set featured photos of name signs that my dad took of
each town we went through all the way up old Highway 27,

through Mackinaw City and to Thessalon, Canada. I learned that it isn't just experiencing an event that is fun – it is the anticipation and the review that makes it extra special. Watching the slides with popcorn and a fire going, the family together, anticipating the next vacation, was almost as good as the vacation.

Both of my parents were outstanding students. I wasn't. I loved to read; I just never read the books I was supposed to read at the time they were assigned. I was always active in journalism, music, and politics. At one point at IPFW, I think I was in 20 different organizations. At Leo High School, during my senior year, I chaired four of the six Student Council committees. At the end of each grade period, my dad would sit down, sad of heart, and wonder if I should join the military to get some discipline. He would pull out his grade card, "Oh, yes, I got a 'B' once, but it was at Harvard and the English course was especially hard." I would feel bad for maybe even several days before reverting back to my old ways. Now his comments seem so wise. I find myself saying the same things to my kids. And hoping they will listen better than I did.

WARM FUZZIES

Maretia C. Temple

My favorite time of the day as a child was Sunday morning. Mom would cook breakfast, and we kids would pile into bed with Dad to read funnies and drink coffee (the only time we got coffee). We would talk about our week, make plans, and giggle a lot.

One of my favorite pastimes in childhood was going to the lake. Every year we would go to Lake Tippecanoe for the summer. We cleaned, painted, etc., for one week and the rest of the summer we played. My Mom and Aunt would cook "summer" food. We would swim and boat all day and play board games or cards at night. Dads came on the weekends and we would ski or go scuba diving. Our parents would put the "record player" on the porch and teach us to dance in the yard. My parents worked very hard, and this was the only time they (and we) really cut loose – it was a totally warm and fuzzy time.

As an adult, I realize how my parents were very accepting people. They were open-minded and caring. This meant there were always a lot of people in our home. Sometimes I resented this, but today I realize what a rich and diverse childhood this gave me.

Though I learned many lessons as a child, honesty and integrity were constantly taught and reinforced. My parents used every teachable moment to its fullest.

As a teenager I realized that life doesn't always go the way you plan, and that you need to be flexible. My Dad died when I was in 7th grade. My Mom was left with a house full of kids to raise. She worked both a full and a part-time job to make ends meet. She also went back to school so she could have a more secure future for us. My role changed from being a free-spirited, kind of goofy teen to that of a responsible "mother substitute" for my younger siblings. I am grateful today – it taught me so much.

As an adult I've come to understand how roles change over time. My mother was seriously injured and my stepfather was killed in a car accident in 1985. Suddenly, I became the caregiver instead of the receiver. I had to learn to value my mother for who she is now, cherish memories, and let go of my own emotional neediness. This was tough, but it has helped me grow tremendously.

Looking back at the people in my life, I treasure so many things. My mom loved enormously. She is soft and smells like dusting powder. My dad loved unconditionally. He was soft to touch, but his hand held you tight. My Grandma Ellen was funny and poetic. My Grandpa Roy was serious and always teaching. I didn't know my other grandparents.

My adopted Aunt Ethel was my favorite aunt; she was generous and always was teaching me things. I always had the best leaf and rock collections because she loved to explore and educate me.

KICK THE CAN

Melvin G. Bozell

When I was a kid, I loved summer mornings. It was cooler before Noon, and it made playing games like "Kick The Can" with my buddy, Eddie Trustie, more fun. Eddie and I loved to play Kick The Can. We used to get all the neighborhood kids who were real slow together and play because we knew they couldn't catch up with us. Sometimes I felt sorry for the slow kids and would let myself get caught – that way they'd keep playing. By evening, it usually was just Eddie and me playing against each other. Those were the days!!

"The memories of one's youth make for
long, long thoughts."

Finnish Proverb

I AM BLESSED

Pat P. Pruis

My parents were always very involved in my life. Being as I was their only child that may seem natural, however there is the risk of "over" involvement. That was not the case with me. I have so many wonderful recollections of my childhood! In no particular order, here are some favorite memories from my youth.

* Going to Maine for summer vacations. Many "firsts" occurred here including: catching my first fish, learning to swim, learning to water ski, hiking, playing tennis, eating lobster, picking blueberries, and my first kiss!

* Sundays after church when my parents would take me to an empty parking lot and teach me to drive the car.

* Riding with the top down in our convertible.

* Mom preparing a special lunch for my teacher. (We walked to school and came home at lunch in those days!)

* Going snow skiing with my parents.

* Having a secret "hand squeeze code" with my Dad that told us that we loved each other "thissssssss much!"

* Putting on plays with my friends and having all our parents sit through them.

* Getting wheel barrel rides from my Dad.

* Spending time with my grandparents, who lived near us for years.

I am blessed to have great parents who encouraged me

to be anything I wanted to be, go anywhere I wanted to go, and always try new things. Thanks, Mom & Dad.

"Every day of your life is a page of your history."

Arabian Proverb

THE B.B. GUN FACTOR

Melvin G. Bozell

One of the biggest lessons I learned occurred around my 10th or 11th birthday. That's when I received a B.B. gun as a gift. I was real proud of that gun. I shot everything I was allowed to shoot: trees, cans, all kinds of stuff.

Anyway, I was walking with a friend, Ed J., down an alley uptown, and he asked to see the B.B. gun. I let him 'cause I like to share my stuff with people. It made me feel connected with others somehow when I shared with them. However, I learned too late that not all connections are good. By the time I realized what he was doing, Ed shot out the upstairs window of Mr. Sullivan's drug store. Old Sullivan spotted us and we ran.

As I ran, I thought how there were two Ed's in my life: Eddie T. and Ed J. Eddie T. kept me out of trouble and Ed J. led me into trouble. Right then, I regretted being with Ed J.

Mr. Sullivan called my Dad down to the drug store and told him that I shot the window (because he saw me carrying the gun). Mr. Sullivan really didn't believe I did the actual shooting, as he knew I was with Ed J., but he wanted the window fixed.

Well, Dad made good with Mr. Sullivan on the window. Boy, was Dad unhappy with me. I told him that I didn't shoot the windows out, Ed did. But he said that he was going to teach me a lesson I wouldn't forget for a long time.

He explained even though the gun was not in my hands at the time the window was shot, it was still my responsibility because I let Ed use the gun.

I was not allowed to have my precious B. B. gun back for a whole year. A whole year! It was a serious punishment, but it helped me realize that I was lucky Ed J. didn't shoot a person or an animal or something that was unfixable. Today, I am very careful about lending my things to others, and I have no guns in my home.

"When you teach your son, you teach your son's son."
The Talmud

HOW QUICKLY THEY LEARN

Jerri Lerch

There are some great advantages to being professionally trained in mental health and psychology while raising children. I've enjoyed a greater understanding of some of their developmental stages. As a result, the "terrible twos" weren't so terrible. We thoroughly enjoyed the all-out enthusiasm and joy that two-year-olds bring to a family, particularly as they initially test their own little personal wills.

To avoid the two-year-old's favorite word, "No", we learned to give them small choices at times. To avoid struggles with the morning routine, we would choose two appropriate outfits, hold them up for the child to see, and ask which one the child wanted to wear. This eliminated single outfit rejections or an all-day process of going through every piece of clothing in the dresser. Frequently, we offered similar simple choices between two items for meals, snacks, vegetables, or activities.

One of the disadvantages of being trained in mental health and psychology is that it doesn't take long for children to learn "psycho-babble" at very young ages. I recall multiple times that my miniature munchkins would be sitting or standing in the large basket area of a shopping cart in a check-out line. One of them would hold up a package of gum in one hand and a package of candy in the other, loudly asking me, "Which one of these two would you like to buy for us, Mom?"

CHERISHED MEMORIES

Kathi Conner-Bricker

These are some of my most cherished memories. I hope you enjoy them too.

Early evening was my favorite time of the day because the stars and moon were out. It was so quiet and peaceful.

I used to go to the lake with my Grandma and Grandpa Emrick every summer until I was 7 or 8 years old. It was so much fun! At night we'd camp out on their boat as it rocked us to sleep. We'd catch fireflies and listen to the crickets. My grandparents always listened to me.

My family traveled to a lot of interesting places, and my parents spent a lot of time playing with us. My Mom and I used to sing our hearts out in the car. Our favorite song was "Downtown" by Petula Clark.

One of the most important lessons I learned was that even when people disappoint you or let you down, it is better to be a friend and trust people than to shut yourself off from others. I would have missed some incredible friendships if I didn't open up to others.

Looking back, I realize now that when I was a teenager getting ready to go out on the town, my mother told me to take enough money for a phone call, my own transportation and a companion, it was to keep me safe rather than to control me. Boundaries keep children safe.

As an adult, I realize that people can change. You can

have the experiences as an adult that you missed as a child. I've also learned that even if you forgive, it still is difficult to forget.

My favorite thing about my mom was her smile and sense of humor. She always told us that she loved us – every day! My mother always looked for the silver lining in every cloud.

"Wheresoever you go, go with all your heart."
Confucius

AN ABUNDANCE OF LOVE.

Sr. Elise Kriss, President, University of Saint Francis

I am the oldest of the six children of Marcella and Joseph Kriss. We were raised in the small town of North Judson, Indiana. Being the oldest, I had—or felt—some responsibility for my brothers and sisters at an early age. This was good, as our parents raised all of us to be quite independent and industrious. Since we were a large family, and only my dad worked in the family grocery store, we did not have everything we always wanted. This, too, was good as we now work hard to have what we need and want individually and what is needed to raise our families. We always had plenty to eat, were simply dressed and enjoyed our times together, including dinner each evening.

My religious upbringing was the result of my training in the home and my opportunity to attend the Catholic grade school in our hometown—SS. Cyril and Methodious School. It was staffed by the Sisters of Saint Francis of Perpetual Adoration from Mishawaka, Indiana. (I am currently a member of this religious congregation and am now President of the University of Saint Francis in Fort Wayne, Indiana.) Our parents saw to it that we had a Catholic education, and they were supportive of our desire to receive a post-secondary education though they were not able to fund these decisions. I have a Ph.D., I have a sister with two Master's degrees, another sister with a Master's degree and a brother with a

Bachelor's degree. One of my brothers is currently taking coursework in business administration. Neither of our parents went to college, but they were very good high school students. My Mom was salutatorian of her high school class.

I remember visiting my grandparents often. They lived at the other end of our small town. They managed the family business, and we all helped out at the store as much as we could. Grandma was good at gathering her brothers and sisters—and there were 11 of them—for the holidays and other special events. I often stayed over night with my grandparents and worked as much as I wanted in the grocery store. Maybe this is where my business and management talents first developed!

I have many fond memories of our home life! The most important impression is that even though we did not have an abundance of material goods, we always had the love and care of our parents, both of whom are now deceased. In their honor, we try to gather as a family whenever we can. This is not easy since I have a brother who lives with his family in Salt Lake City and a sister near Richmond, Virginia. Four of us live in northern Indiana, so we frequently get together. My sister and I are also involved in researching our family history to learn more about our ancestors and all their descendants.

I was on the SCAN Board of Directors for several years, and I realize that my childhood memories are very happy compared to some youngsters who are not cared for or loved as they should be by their parents or guardians. It makes me thank God every day for my parents, my brothers and sisters and the love we share as a family.

"The happiest moments of my life have been the few which I have passed at home in the bosom of my family."
Thomas Jefferson

TRADITIONS

Lynn M. Noneman

My mother left me far too soon. She passed away just two months before my 18th birthday. She didn't leave me with very many memories, words of wisdom, good advice, insightful thoughts or the true meaning of life. But she did leave me with traditions, and I have carried these traditions through my life and the lives of my daughters. Now they are carrying them into their families' lives…things like fixing traditional holiday dinners, awaiting Santa's arrival, coloring Easter eggs, carving pumpkins and so on.

Just this year I said to my daughters (now 30 and 25 years old) "Are you tired of hunting for Easter Eggs yet?" They said they would never tire of it. So, once again, we prepared their Easter baskets, filling them with the "girls'" favorite goodies, and carefully hid plastic eggs throughout the house. Even as adults, my daughters enjoy finding these colorful treasures and the surprises in them. I, too, still feel a thrill as I tell them they are "getting warmer" when they're dashing around the house trying to find the eggs. Now my 2-year-old granddaughter joins the hunt! It all begins again.

I wish my mother were here to see what she began. She couldn't have known the impact these events would have on our lives. Traditions! I am grateful to her for having them, because it's a piece of her I will never forget. And neither will my children, and their children, and the children yet to come.

Pause and Reflect

Take a moment and think about your own experiences as a child, parent, or grandparent.

1. What are your favorite childhood memories?

2. What memories of your children's (or nieces, nephews, friends, etc...) childhood do you hope to never forget?

3. What life lessons have you learned from the stories that have been told to you by your family members?

4. When and how do you use stories to help children reflect on fond or important memories of their journey?

CHAPTER 3

MOMS

"I miss thee, my Mother! Thy image is still
The deepest impressed on my heart."

Eliza Cook

If there's one universal truth to motherhood, it has to be that few women are ever the same after they hold their first child. You look at your son or daughter and love them so much you can't imagine ever loving someone so completely. Then, you realize, as days turn into months and months traipse into years, that one day your child will leave you. It hits you that you must let them go and live their own life.

One of the most difficult things a parent learns is to let your children go. To let them fly from you, one little journey at a time. It starts when they first try to wriggle out of your arms. Then when they begin walking. Then their independence seems to just blossom. You'll let go the first time your children spend the night away from home... Their first day of school... When they learn to drive... When they move out on their own. Sometimes it aches so much, but still, you let them go.

One mother remarked that our children will never love us as much as we love them because we would never leave our children, but they will leave us.

Yes. Each stage of motherhood has elements of teaching and loving and letting go. And, as we practice releasing our children into life, we are teaching them how to love us enough to let go when it's our time to say goodbye to this earth.

Thoughts from Rachel

Motherhood came to my life when I was just three months from being 31. I have often told others that I was older, well-educated, mature, and a responsible adult, but nothing, absolutely nothing, had prepared me for motherhood.

I remember so explicitly the first night I was home with my first-born. She cried all night. At about 4:30 in the morning, exhausted, I finally laid down in bed with her stretched out on top of me. I was about to doze off and she wet herself all the way through her diaper, all over my nightgown, and all over the sheets of the bed. I just lay there and thought, "life is never going to be the same again", and "what did I do?" Life has never been the same, and I don't regret one moment of it.

Nothing changed my life or who I was more than becoming a mother. From carefree and playful to responsible and serious, I was transformed from a grown-up "child" to a full-fledged adult. At least that is how it felt to me. It is an overwhelming sense of responsibility for another's life with inadequate knowledge that spurs the change, but it is the love one feels for the child that is the fuel.

Motherhood brought on a whole new kind of love, a love that was felt from the tips of my toes to the top of my head. No feeling I had ever had was as strong. From this love also came the extremes of every other feeling I had experienced in my life. Fear was palpable when the child was in danger, anger was purple with bright red flames, pride at their successes was enough to make my chest burst open. All the emotions of the world became more intense... frustrations, worry, sadness, and joy.

Being awash in these emotions changes a woman and transforms her into someone different than she was before. One of the other surprises was how all of a sudden I could relate anew to the woman I had called Mother. All the sacrifices she had made, all the episodes where she was mean, all the support she had given actively and behind the scenes, were now appreciated. It was much easier to understand her mistakes and her love. It was much easier to understand her wisdom and to ask for her help.

Reflections from Dave

Moms mean "home" to me. When I close my eyes and think about my mother, I recall the family home with all the familiar sights, sounds, smells and the lessons she taught me from that classroom. When I think about my wife, Rosie, and what a wonderful mom she is for our children, I also think of home. Yes, I think that she has been the creator of a space that will forever be remembered as home in the minds of my children. "There is no place like home" is synonymous with "Mom".

As a child, one of my favorite movies was "The Wizard of Oz", and I looked forward to watching it each year. I still recall the first time I saw it on color TV and the magic of the story. Now, I realize it was a story about home and the essential components that often only a mother can create. In the film, Dorothy finds herself in a strange land and goes to great lengths to find her way home. Along the way she meets others who are also looking for something; the scarecrow wants a brain, the lion desires courage, and the tin man searches for a heart. The group sets off for Emerald City to ask the Wizard to help them find all that they seek. Sadly, the Wizard was not who they imagined, and the innocence and trust of Dorothy and her friends is broken. They had risked it all to ask the Wizard to give them the qualities they needed at home: security, love, courage, and wisdom. By closing her eyes, clicking her heels, and repeating "there's no place like home," Dorothy finds herself back on her farm surrounded by the love that had always been there, but that she had sometimes failed to see.

Our moms create a place called home and fill it with love, security, courage, and wisdom. Our mothers become our first nurses, teachers, scientists, explorers, and police. Often we don't appreciate their value during the chaos and challenges of growing up. But behind their "wizardly curtain," mothers work their every day magic to keep the family together. Like glue, these bonding properties, though always present, often go unrecognized.

There really is no place like home. As an adult I realize the security, love, courage, and wisdom I have today was created by Mom.

REMINISCING WITH MOM

Patricia L. Slocum

I went to visit my parents this past Easter weekend. Due to home and work issues, I had not seen them for over eight months. This time I did not have to accompany a frantic dog nor a teenage son with a driver's permit who insisted on driving part of the 600 mile trip! Sans dog and son, I had more time to think on the long drive, as well as take a trip down memory lane because my parents now live close to where I grew up. I had not visited this place for more than 20 years.

Mom and I did some sightseeing. We drove by our old house and my high school. That night after dinner, we continued to reminisce about my high school years. I was amazed at the "black holes" in my memory – things I can't quite remember but were significant enough for others to recall as if they'd occurred yesterday. Mom had one such memory that I'll share.

As far back as I can remember, I had told everyone that my dream was to attend Syracuse University and become a writer. In my junior year of high school, I had been accepted to Syracuse, and I just assumed that I'd be able to go. Mom said that one night I sat down at the kitchen table and put together a financial plan that would enable me to attend Syracuse. She said that she was amazed at how organized, creative and positive I was that it would all fall together. (It did by the way.) She went on to say that, not only was she proud of me for making my dream come true, but that she wished she had been more like me. Mom told me that she feels I'm a person who goes out and makes things happen, while she sees herself as the opposite. As she told me this story I could picture the kitchen table, how I must have looked putting the pencil to the paper! I could imagine it, but I didn't remember it.

So it was my turn to be amazed by how my mother felt about herself! My mom balanced a nursing career, a demanding husband and three children. We never wanted for anything. She was the glue that held us all together. And all this time, she thought I was taking after my Dad who was an executive with an insurance company. Mom made it happen for me. From her nurturing, I have become a proud mother of two successful sons. From her example of parenting, I have become a better parent. And thank goodness she now knows.

BIRDY

Marcia J. Laker

Lay your head on me, babe
Allow me to caress your brow
How sweet and fleet the hours be
On the maternal bough.

From the book of poems titled
Recent Sightings
MINC Publishing
2002
Reprinted with permission.

"A mother's arms are made of tenderness and children sleep soundly in them."
Victor Hugo

NATURE'S WONDERS

Mary Ann Bleeke

One of the greatest gifts my parents gave me was a love
of nature. They raised me on 13 acres of land filled with trees,
ravines and my very own creek. Although Mom was quite
over-protective of me, she would let me go to the creek on my
own as long as my dog went with me.

During my childhood summers, Mom regularly would
pack me a picnic lunch (complete with hot dogs for my dog)
and off Princess and I would go! We ventured to the woods
and creek, rock hopping, wading, and catching crawdads and
grasshoppers.

I always thought it strange that a woman who wouldn't
let me cross the road alone would let me go off to the creek.
But Mom was really good about letting nature take its course,
bandaging knees, giving a hug and making sure I always kept
right on going, never allowing anything to get in the way of
my fun in the woods.

During those years, I always picked wild trilliums from
the woods for Mother's Day. Now as an adult, riding my bike
through another woods that I love, I am struck by the sight of
the trilliums. I pause and remember how my Mom encouraged
my love of nature and helped foster my sense of exploration
and adventure. Perhaps that's one of the reasons I could move,
by myself, away from my hometown and know that I would be
okay. Nature (and the memory of Mom) is always with me.

They Grow Up So Fast

Adrienne M. Clark

It was late in the fall in 1960. I was rocking and enjoying my new baby. I had just finished breast feeding him and simply was relaxing and enjoying the moment when the mail came. I opened a card from my sister to find a note from her scribbled at the bottom. "Enjoy your baby," she'd written. "They grow up faster than you think."

I never have forgotten her words of advice and enjoyed every one of my children in every one of their various stages. Now I pass that same piece of advice on to new parents whenever I can. As a trainer for the Healthy Families program at SCAN, I have the opportunity to do this daily, as I teach our home visiting team how to mentor new parents. *"Enjoy your babies, they grow up faster then you think"* is a message of hope they are sharing with each new parent they see.

More Than A Name

Lynn M. Noneman

The greatest gift I've ever received isn't a diamond or money or any material thing. It's a baby girl by the name of Isabelle Lynn. My granddaughter! Now, I know a lot of grandparents think their grandchild is the best, but I know Isabelle is special. She carries the name of my mother.

My mother died when I was 17. She never saw my first car, met my husband, danced at my wedding or experienced the birth of my daughters. I felt cheated. She never knew her granddaughters. She never had a chance to really know me!

When my daughter told me I was going to be a grandmother, I was thrilled and sad at the same time. If only my mother could be here. Then, Cherise told me that she and her husband had decided to name a daughter after my mother and me. Any sense of sadness disappeared as I hugged her.

For the next eight months, I was afraid to hope for a girl for fear I'd be disappointed. I had to leave this in God's hands. But on that wonderful day in September, God blessed us with the most beautiful, most perfect baby girl. When I walked into my daughter's hospital room and saw her holding this bundle of joy, she said, "Meet your granddaughter, Isabelle Lynn".

Life does go on. The circle has been completed. That little girl carries more than just a name to me. The spirit of what was lost has been reborn and lives on.

IN THE DRIVER'S SEAT

Eleanor H. Marine

One of my fondest memories of Mother concerns her need to quit driving at the age of 90. She began experiencing a glare problem with her eyes and, for safety's sake, stopped driving a car. Despite this setback, Mother continued to go to work each day at a family rug shop. My brother, who lived with her, would drive her to the store each morning, then turn around and pick her up a few hours later and bring her home.

I once asked Mother if she hoped to solve her eye problem and resume driving. She looked at me as if I had lost my mind and said, "Of course I hope to drive again. Actually," she said, "I never quit. When your brother brings me home, I send him off and get in the car and drive around the neighborhood. I don't want to lose my skills."

What a spirit!

A GENEROUS MOTHER

Stephanie Jentgen

I know an incredible woman. From the moment I met her when we were co-workers at Seyfert's Potato Chips, I knew she was a unique person. But the depths of her generosity and unconditional love for her daughter would not be fully revealed to me until years later.

This woman has not had an easy adult life. At the age of 20 she married her soul mate, and within a couple years, they had a beautiful daughter. Sadly, her husband sank into the hell of alcoholism. This woman did all she could to help him try to sober up, but there was nothing in her power that could change his destiny. Despite her love for him, this woman had to leave. Being a single mom was difficult. Though this woman had a loving, supportive family, she still struggled with being both mother and father to her little girl.

When I met Marybeth Lomont, I was a college student working at Seyfert's to help with tuition. She was a full-timer, about 10 years older than me, who took every bit of overtime to make sure her daughter's needs, and wants, were met. Marybeth and I became good friends. Not only did we socialize with other co-workers, she invited me into her life and introduced me to her daughter, Janell. Watching her with Janell was wonderful – they had such a good relationship. Sure, Janell would try to push "MB's" buttons, but you could tell that this little girl knew she was loved and that her mom would always put her first.

MB and I stayed in touch throughout my college years and beyond. We had a lot of fun together, and I thought she was the greatest. You always knew where you stood with MB — she was honest and forthright. If she was upset with me, she'd let me know. But she always encouraged me to work hard toward my dreams. She constantly would say, "You don't want to end up like me, working in a factory." I hated to hear her say that about herself because I thought so highly of her. I really had no clue how hard she struggled to give her daughter a good life.

I would find out, though, many years down the road.

In 1992, I met someone named Denny Lomont. I figured he must be a relative of Marybeth. One evening, I heard him tell his life story to a group of people in treatment to recover from alcoholism. His story seemed oddly familiar. He told how his alcoholism destroyed his marriage and that the wife he loved had to leave him for her safety and that of her daughter. He spoke of how his drinking robbed him of his health and severely damaged a heart that genetics predisposed to trouble. Denny's eyes misted up as he remembered laying in the hospital, waiting for a heart transplant, and a blond, blue-eyed little girl bounced onto his bed and said, "Hi, Dad" and proceeded to show him a photo album of the years he had missed in her life.

All of a sudden it hit me. This was Marybeth's ex-husband. He was the drunk that had left her so sad. He was the subject of so many talks that she and I had shared. But now he was sober and trying to help others change their lives. He helped me change mine.

Denny and I became friends. I still maintained contact with Marybeth, and she thought it was quite a coincidence that I met her ex-husband.

Over the years, I became more and more involved with Freedom House, the halfway house where Denny was the director. Eventually I was elected to its Board of Directors. And Denny and I became closer. One day, we realized that what had begun as a friendship had blossomed into true love.

Of course, I wondered how Marybeth would feel about this turn of events. Though she and Denny had been divorced for years and were friendly, I wasn't sure how she would react to me as his mate.

I didn't need to worry. Though she was surprised, Marybeth was supportive, kind and non-judgmental. Even more, she welcomed me back into her life not just as a friend, but as a potential stepmother for her daughter. You see, Marybeth still put Janell first. She wanted her daughter to be happy, and she knew that Janell and Denny had worked hard to re-establish a relationship. The last thing MB was going to do was stand in the way of Janell's happiness. I'd like to think that our friendship, and the fact that I'd known Janell since she was a young girl, helped put her at ease.

To this day, Marybeth still treats me as one of the family. This has been an incredible gift to me. Denny died of cancer on Christmas morning of 1998. He and I were supposed to be married just 12 hours later, but God called him home before that. I'm grateful that he and I exchanged wedding rings about four hours before he died; something told both of us that he might not make it through the night.

From the moment he passed away, Marybeth has continued to be supportive. She continues to include me in family holidays, family gatherings, and she introduces me as Janell's stepmother. This woman has no reason to do this, she just does. I don't believe she knows how grateful I am to have her in my life. I cannot have children, so Janell is the only daughter I'll ever know. Because of Marybeth's love, generosity and friendship, she has shared her precious child with me.

So this story is a tribute to one of the most amazing women I know: Marybeth Lomont. May you always be showered with the love and kindness that you have bestowed upon me.

DOG GONE BROTHERS

Jennifer Boen

As far back as I can remember, my mother told me this story. It still makes me smile when I think of it.

My mother was nine months pregnant with me. My brothers were ages three and four. In those last days before I was born, my brothers decided to "pull every trick in the book of orneriness." They greased their tricycles with tractor axle grease, put rocks in the corn planter (it was May, and my farmer father was planting crops then) and did a myriad of other things. The last straw for my mother occurred when she found Garrett, 3, eating the dog's food.

When questioned, he told my mother that his brother (Robert, 4) made him eat it. She discovered that Robert also had munched through several handfuls of the pooch's dinner. My mother, a nurse, grabbed the boys and took them to the bathroom, where she gave them each an enema, hoping to get the nasty stuff out of their system as fast as possible before any harm was done.

While one boy sat on the toilet, and the other on the little potty, Mom sat on the floor. She began reading the ingredient list on the side of the dog food box: riboflavin, niacin, vitamins A, D, B, C, iron, etc. "I had a notion to feed them some more," she told people later.

My mother was a wonderful, creative woman who continues to be a role model for me, although she died more than 20 years ago. She taught me that a sense of humor is essential as a parent.

"The mother's heart is the child's schoolroom."
Henry Ward Beecher

An Extraordinary Woman

Craig Bobay

I am happy to recognize an extraordinary parent, my wife, Nancy Ann Bobay. When I think of Nancy's most outstanding qualities, I think of her passion and compassion. She approaches everything in her life with unusual energy and graceful dedication. She simply is the most extraordinary and wonderful person I have ever met. Nancy has made my most difficult job, that of being a parent, much easier than most people experience.

Nancy and I first met back in the early 1970s in high school. Shortly after I met her, I noticed that people of all ages, ethnicity, and abilities just seemed to have a natural liking and admiration for Nancy. Although I was easily attracted by her strawberry-blond hair and physical beauty, as I came to know her better, it was other, intangible attributes of real beauty that caused me to fall hopelessly in love with Nancy. Then, as now, those virtues – Nancy's spirituality, strong sense of family, sense of humor, easy laugh, and genuine concern for others (especially for those most in need), make her easy to cherish.

Contrary to the values of the "me generation" that were sweeping our culture and campuses at that time, Nancy enrolled in college with the goal of learning skills so that she could benefit people who were traditionally cast aside by the larger society. While college students, Nancy and I both worked weekends as house parents in residential training programs for developmentally disabled adults. Nancy flourished in the position, and with her encouragement, I, too, learned a great deal about the humanity, true strengths, and value of the people whom we served, who happened to be a little different from me. I also quickly learned that Nancy would almost always become an instant favorite of the residents. Over the years, Nancy has continued to be held in such high esteem by them and by her peers who also serve them.

Any fears I had about raising children in our troubling times were set aside by knowing that Nancy would bring the same qualities to parenthood as she did to her professional calling. So, we went down the path to parenthood with our eyes wide open and with confidence that with good judgment, common sense, the support of our extended families, and our faith community, we would handle being parents.

Now, 23 years after the birth of our first child, we have three beautiful daughters (who are fortunate to have their mother's good looks). They all have been a joy to watch as they grew and learned. The girls are devoted to their mom. Nancy has made sure that each of our daughters makes the most of their God-given talents. Every night Nancy worked with them on their homework assignments to make sure the girls developed the intellectual skills necessary to make contributions to our community as adults. She's also made sure the girls have learned to enjoy life (and to enjoy the special bond that develops between mothers and daughters through frequent excursions to the mall)! She is the role model every girl needs.

Even after challenging days at work, Nancy makes the girls her priority, ensuring they get the love and attention they need to succeed. Remarkably, Nancy also did all of this while working full-time, all by herself for three years (when our oldest was in first grade, and her sister was a newborn) while I went away to law school at Indiana University in Bloomington, Indiana. While I was 200 miles away, deep in stacks of law books, Nancy kept our family together. During that challenging time, Nancy provided the girls (and me) with love, food and shelter, encouragement, and faith in our future, while always making sure that we enjoyed life. Being with her is almost always fun. Nancy's smile and sense of fun always have helped me and the girls get through life's bumps.

Nancy also has made sure that our family has kept God at the center of our lives. With her support and encouragement, our faith as a family has continued to grow. We thank God for giving her to us.

In becoming such a good, loving parent, Nancy has had the good fortune of many excellent examples in both her and my families. Nancy's parents, Gus and Millie Verstynen, also were devoted to their children and church. And although they were both called home to our Lord early in their lives, their positive influence on Nancy (and through her, on me and the girls) as excellent parents has been priceless.

Luckily, both of us had shining examples of loving, caring, involved, and giving parents. My parents, Tom and Joan Bobay, have provided Nancy and me with love and support since I first brought her home to them in 1974. Our brothers, sisters, aunts, uncles, cousins, and many good friends have likewise been great sources of support for us as parents, and all have admired Nancy's grace and humor.

Nancy's personal and professional life choices over the 27 years of our marriage have provided an excellent example for our three daughters. Nancy's way of loving and of treating all people with dignity will live on through our daughters long after we are gone. As to her lighter side, I also see Nancy's sense of humor in the girls. Let's face it, a guy who lives with four women has to appreciate a sense of humor in them! All four of them are fun to be around.

To me, Nancy's life perfectly illustrates what people mean when they speak of compassion and passion. For Beth, Mollie and Annie, I thank her. I'm grateful to have the opportunity to share these thoughts about my best friend, my cherished life companion, and my daughters' loving mom.

MARCHING ORDERS

Mary Ann Bleeke

My mother was a woman with high expectations combined with a critical and demanding nature. She always made it clear that you finished your work before you were allowed to play, and things had to be done "right", acting much as I imagined she did as a First Lieutenant in the Army during World War II. (My mother truly was a feminist before the term was coined!) As she aged, however, the "marching orders" increased. Sadly, so did her own frustration and anger at her physical limitations. You see, she became wheelchair bound, and she often projected her anger on those who were the closest to her. As an only child, that usually meant I was in the line of fire, along with a good friend, or two, who took the time to be close to me.

One time, a very dear friend accompanied my mother and me on a trip to visit a dying family member. Mother was in her prime, barking orders at us, needing this or that immediately all day long. My friend and I simply attended to her needs, rolling our eyes behind her back a time or two. Yet at the end of the day, tucked safely in her bed, Mom was able to bark a final order of the day to both of us, "Now, come here and give me a kiss good night. I love you both!"

With such a change, she could melt my heart and remind me again of the unconditional love that had always been there, but often was covered with the frustrations of her own dependence. How I wish I could have overlooked that anger more often to see the love behind it.

"I'm not afraid of storms,
for I'm learning to sail my ship.""
Louisa May Alcott

LIFE IS LIKE A BOX OF POP-TARTS....

Melissa Long

I have an older brother whom I dearly love. He was three years ahead of me in school. Whenever my brother would bring home a yearbook, I spent hours gazing at the girls in the pictures. The cheerleaders, the homecoming queens, the violin players fascinated me. I decided that, when I went to high school, I was going to be the girl in those pictures! My name would be the most frequently mentioned in the yearbook!

My mom, who always completely supported my endeavors, dutifully hauled me to violin lessons, piano lessons, singing practice, and anything else I wanted to do. By the time I started my first day of high school, I was ready to make my dreams come true. The first step in my plan to have the most frequent mention in the yearbook was to try out for cheerleading. I succeeded and became part of the cheerleading squad. After that came the school play, the orchestra, the speech team, the student council... I tried just about everything; and everything I tried, I accomplished. My photos in the yearbook were going to be so numerous even I would be impressed; though I had long forgotten my original goal in the pursuit of all of those activities.

In my junior year, I was going for the big enchilada: Class President. My mother knew how much I wanted to add this prize to my resume. She and Dad really pulled for me. The time came for me to deliver my speech over the PA system, and I was great! In the voting, I swept all challengers. On the way home from school, I was eager to see what my parents would say. I knew Mom must be planning a surprise for me if I won. What would it be? I waltzed through the door, triumphantly announcing my victory. My mom hugged me and congratulated me and told me how proud she was. She then went to the cupboard and pulled out a box of Pop-Tarts. "Here, I got these for you!" Now, I loved Pop-Tarts... but this was it?! My big reward?!

"Gee mom", I said. "That's not a very big prize!"

Mom replied, "Actually, I got these for you in case you lost. I know how much you love them." And with that, my mother returned to her stove to continue fixing supper.

It took me a while to appreciate what a gift my mom had given me. She wasn't telling me that my accomplishment wasn't worth much. She was telling me that success isn't measured by what you do, so much as by who you are. She was telling me that she loved me just the same whether I'd won or lost. It's a lesson I never forgot.

We all want our children to be winners. We imagine them as successful students, athletes, achievers. Sometimes they let us down. It's easy to win; it's hard to lose. But if we show our kids that we love them no matter what, they will learn grace in victory and grace in defeat. It's an attitude that came in handy my freshman year in college, when my picture was in the yearbook only once.

WHAT IS A "MOTHER?"

Mary Ann Buckel

Does a woman have to give birth to a child to be a mother? The dictionary says a mother is a "female parent, a woman looked upon as a mother who has authority over a child. A term of endearment used for an elderly woman. A person that shows maternal affection, a person that exercises protective care over someone else." So does this make me a mother? I think so, in all the ways that really count.

I never had children of my own, but I helped raise two little boys for my father-in-law. I was 17 years old, had just finished high school and knew nothing about keeping house and raising children. However, I quickly learned how to manage a home, cook, clean and be a "mother" and a wife. I learned to love and care for someone besides myself.

If a mother is the person who changes the diapers, fixes the food, gives the baths and loves the children as her own, then what else does a mother need to be?

The joyful memories of those days in my life have lasted until this day. Paul and Patrick were the only redeeming features in a home I felt was filled with chaos. I was married to their brother who was 25 years their senior. My marriage was turbulent; my husband and his father both drank heavily. I tried to keep the children safe, but could not always keep their father from mistreating them. That broke my heart, and I overcompensated by spoiling them as much as I could. I remember sitting up all night rocking the children when they were sick. I would sing to them and tell them stories about dragons and princes. Their father re-married in 1972 and moved to Washington state, taking the children with them.

I thought I was going to die from the pain I felt at their father taking them away. That feeling is still as strong today as it was all those years ago. Does loving a child so much your insides almost fall out from the pain make a mother? I think it does.

Recently I underwent serious surgery and have been feeling my own mortality. I have been reminiscing about my life with the children. I called them last night to get their opinion of what a mother was to them. I only have talked to them a few times since they have grown up, and my heart still leaped out of my chest at the sound of their voices. Does this make me a mother? I think it does.

A mother makes the sacrifices needed to ensure that the children in her care are safe and secure.

Is a mother still a mother if she abuses her children and neglects them? In my work, I have seen the most abused child still light up when her mother enters a room. Children are so forgiving of so many things. It makes me wonder if parents really understand the gift they have been given simply by being loved and accepted by their children. I have observed very few children who rejected their parents, regardless of the severity of the abuse or neglect. What is that bond that transcends everything and causes the child to have a need for their mother?

When I was 21, I found my real family. I had been separated from them for 21 years due to no fault of their own. My heart ached to have my mother hold me and stroke my hair. I was a grown woman, yet I still needed my mother.

A mother is the person that a child needs to complete their life and feel safe in the world. A mother is the person that your heart yearns for until you are finally held and feel loved. A mother is the person who holds a dream for 25 years that her child will be successful and be happy. A mother is the person that calls her boys and tells them that they were the joy of her life and always will be.

All these things are what make a woman a mother. Any female can have a baby, even an animal has babies. A mother is the one that gives her heart without asking anything in return, treasures all that a child gives back, and has the eternal hope that her child will have brighter tomorrows.

PAUSE AND REFLECT

Take a moment and think about your own experiences with
your mother, your child or your grandchild.

1. What are your fondest memories of your mother?

2. When you close your eyes and drift back in thought to
your earlier childhood memories, what are some of the sights,
sounds, colors, and smells that your recall?

3. What lessons do you recall that your mother taught you about security? Love? Courage? Wisdom?

4. As a mother, grandmother, or stepmother today, what memories or lessons do you want your children to recall about you?

CHAPTER 4

DADS

"Any man can be a father.
It takes someone special to be a dad."
Author Unknown

Children need their fathers. History and society in the past often discounted or minimized this important role. Perhaps this is because mothers were deemed the nurturers, the homemakers, and the "child care" workers in the family. One of the best results of the women's movement of the 1970s when many women assumed increasing roles in the work world, was the role of father began to be seen in new light. Men were encouraged to be fathers who were more than " bread winners" and to have increasingly interactive relationships with their children. Fathers provide values, skills, and perspective on life that every child needs. Fathers can balance child rearing. They play gregariously and worry about different things than mom. They let children explore without letting them go too soon. They love deeply, but differently than mothers.

Thoughts from Rachel

The joke in my family is that each of us was "Dad's favorite". In reality I was his favorite. At least in every memory I have I was the favorite. My father died when I was 21, so I was never able to be an adult viewing him as an adult. His death, though, left a wound that has been 30 years healing. He was nurturing, kind, and affectionate. There was nothing like having him come up beside me and give me a hug, take his pipe out of his mouth and kiss me on my cheek. At the same time he could put me in my place with fewer words than anyone I know. After my first quarter at college, my grades came. They were not stellar to say the least. At that point in time, grades came home to parents, not the student. The night they arrived by "snail" mail, he opened them. He looked at them. He came and found me. He handed them to me and said, "Are you proud of these?" He didn't say another word. He walked out. Every quarter after that my grades met the mark of something I could be proud.

Divorce made me even more aware how important fathers are. When a couple divorces, the personal pain of loss, of failure, of anger and disappointment are so acute that it is hard to see beyond oneself. It was during this time of personal trauma that I heard two things that have stuck with me. My children's father said, " What I miss the most is the ability to kiss my children goodnight each evening." His feelings, his love for his children had gotten dismissed in our anguish as a couple. Not long after that my mother said to me, "No one took your father away from you; don't take your girls' father away from them." I was angry with her at the time, but the words rang constantly in my mind. My mother knew how important my dad had been and wanted to make sure I remembered that is how my children felt about their father.

Reflections from Dave

Several weeks before my father died from throat cancer, I was able to sit with him and ask him questions about his life journey. I asked him to reflect on his life and share with me the lessons that he learned along the way. He had already taught me many life lessons, but this time I took notes and hung onto every word he said. I knew that the gift I would receive from him would be well thought out and deeply rooted in faith. We sat closely in the Lazy Boy chairs of our family home where I grew up. I'm sure we had coffee, and I held my journal and pen closely as he meandered through memories.

As Dad reflected back, he told stories and lessons that he had learned from his parents. He explained that back in his day his mother would scold him if he cried. He recalled her words, "Don't cry, little boys don't cry… if you want something to cry about… I'll give you something, now go on and get out of here…" Although Dad heard the message "don't cry", his life passage taught him different. He explained, "It is okay to cry… to have feelings… and express them… but then it's important to move on… 'get out of here'… his mother's words… so to speak."

Dad also reflected cautiously that today he tries to "let go of anger" a little bit earlier… He recalled the words of his father to his mother. "Oh, Ethel… that doesn't amount to no more than a hill of beans." In other words don't sweat the small stuff. Dad said he prayed for the lessons of anger and not sweating the small stuff.

Dad reflected on many of life's challenges in the time we spent together. He summarized the importance of living one day at a time, putting God first, crying if needed, moving on from old hurts and anger, and not sweating the small stuff. Dad said many of the things he "sweated over" earlier in his life were the "small stuff."

"When you are a father,
and you hear your children's voices,
you will feel that those little ones are akin
to every drop in your veins;
that they are the very flower of your life
and you will cleave so closely to them
that you seem to feel
every movement that they make."
Honore De Balzaac (1799-1850)
From *Le Pere Goriot*

DADDY'S GIRL

Judy Pursley

It took Dad many years to decide to marry and raise a family, but once his mind was made up, he was the best father this awkward, pigeon-toed girl could have. He literally ran home from his day's labors to sing and play with me. He spent endless hours reading fairy tales while I snuggled into his lap.

My memories suggest that he taught me all of the essential life-skills — how to spiral a football, ride a two-wheeler, skin-the-cat on the monkey bars, and paint a birdhouse. Though he never knew it, he also taught me patience, a good work ethic, loyalty, and trusting love.

As a child, I worried that I would lose him because he was an "old" dad. Thankfully, his greatest gift to me was that he lived to be 92 years old. My last words to him were, "I've loved you every day of my life, Daddy."

"Certain is it that there is no kind of affection so purely angelic as of a father to a daugther."
Joseph Addison

An Outstanding Father

Karen Roberts

When I met Gerry 12 years ago, one of the qualities
I found most attractive was his dedication as a father. His
children were 21, 19 and 16 years old at the time. Four
years prior, a tragic auto accident had sent the middle child
to hospitals for two years and had sparked a contentious
divorce. In the aftermath, Gerry had primary custody of the
children, including the daily supervision of his brain-injured
son. His career path was frozen as he struggled to meet his job
responsibilities while managing his children's needs.

Today, we have been married for eight years. The
eldest child is now a wife and mother of two young children
and works part-time as a hospital nurse near her home in
Florida. She talks to her dad at least twice a week for practical
advice and emotional support. Gerry went to Florida for two
weeks one winter to help with the kids while she recovered
from surgery.

Gerry's younger son is now married, the father of a
small boy with another on the way. When he was a teenager,
he wasn't looking for advice or instruction in practical skills.
He was busy fending for himself while his dad was occupied
with his injured brother. Today he frequently consults his dad
on topics ranging from finances to household repairs. They
have undertaken many home improvement projects together.

With the exception of alternate weekends, David,

the injured son, is with us every day. His dad wakes him each morning and takes him to catch the bus to the sheltered workshop where he spends his weekdays. Usually David is docile and has a sense of humor. When he becomes upset about something, his dad can divert him with a joke and he quickly forgets whatever bothered him. At 31, he has the faith in his father that most 10-year-old's exhibit. After 16 years of enduring the heartbreak of his son's lost potential, Gerry's devotion to David's care has never flagged. Is there any greater test for a parent? In my eyes, Gerry has passed this test of love and faith with flying colors.

"We find delight in the beauty and happiness of children that makes the heart too big for the body."
Ralph Waldo Emerson
From *The Conduct of Life*

SANTA CAN BE REAL

Rachel Tobin-Smith

We read a lot about the impact parents can have on us in a short time. As parents, when we make mistakes, we tend to berate ourselves or blow the incident off and think we aren't that important in our child's life. A good friend once taught me a way to view these mistakes. She said, "Parenting is like a bank. As long as you are putting in more than you are taking out, you will be alright."

This has really born in on me as the 30th anniversary of my father's death has drawn near. It seems a lifetime ago, yet he taught me so much… so many lessons learned from a man who was only in my life until I was 21. Some of these lessons were given through words of wisdom. Things like, "Always make the person you are with feel as if they are the most important person in the world." "Never quit because it is hard." After my first quarter in college and my report came home with a not-so-wonderful 2.4 average, my father turned to me, handed it over and asked, "Are you proud of this?" He then walked out of the room. After that, the only time I received a grade below a 'B' was the spring semester he died.

Some of the lessons came through his one-on-one time with me. My dad was a Russian-Jewish immigrant. My mother was Irish-Catholic. We celebrated all the holidays in our home - Christmas, Hanukkah, Easter, Passover… One Christmas holiday, when I was still very little, my anticipation of Santa's coming was threatened by rumors that Santa wasn't real. When it came time for bedtime that night, my father took me up on his knee. I was worrying and fretting about the whole Santa issue. I was upset and couldn't go to sleep. My father listened hard. He finally told me a story from when he was little (so he said). He told me that one Christmas Eve he hid under the table in his parents' kitchen. He said that deep into the night he was awakened by a lot of noise and rattling. He opened his eyes and he saw Santa unloading his bag of toys. I was thrilled! I was relieved! I quickly hopped into bed and slept soundly, sure that Santa would visit me just as he visited my dad.

Years later, when I had my own children and my father already was long-dead, this story came back to me. I remembered the security I felt being in his arms, the relief I felt from his reassurance and how this little white "fib" had been just the right thing at the right time to help me through this stage. As I was thinking of all of this, something greater dawned on me... my father was Jewish! Santa never came to his house. I chuckled to myself at this realization. He chose to move past what and who he was at the time to make me the most important person in the world to him. Now some of you might say that he lied to me and we shouldn't teach children to lie. And he did lie to me. But now that I have been a parent for more than 20 years, I realize that there are many times I have told my children that "everything is going to work out" when I really wasn't sure. I realized that at different ages children can handle different spoonfuls of reality. My father realized at the time that a preschooler needed to believe in the magic of Christmas, the spirit of giving represented by Santa. As such, he gave me this story.

"Blessed indeed is the man who hears many gentle voices call him father!"
Lydia M. Child
from *Philothea: A Romance, 1836*

THE BEST OF TIMES —
THE WORST OF TIMES

Lynn M. Noneman

I was Dad's favorite. All the other kids knew it, too. I was the fourth of five children. Dad was partial to me because I tried harder... to fit in, to be noticed by him. I took an interest in what Dad was interested in. Baseball... I could rattle off stats like ERA's, strike outs, batting averages and more. Football... I got to meet Gale Sayers once. I was the only girl there. Basketball... Go Bulls!

So when the doctors diagnosed Dad with cancer and told him he only had six months to live, there was no question that he would live out the time he had left with me. With the wonderful, loving support of my husband and family, I embarked on the hardest, yet the most rewarding, challenge of my life. Dad did not make it six months. He only lived six weeks. During that time, he was afraid to go to sleep at night for fear he wouldn't wake up. So, we stayed up all night talking about everything and anything. During one of those all-night sessions he must have felt pretty good because at five o'clock in the morning he asked me if I'd get him a beer and a hot dog with onions. At the time I thought it was a strange request... but later on it seemed like the right choice. The look on his face and the glimmer in his eyes made it all worthwhile.

Caring for my dad in his final days may have been the

hardest thing I've had to do in my life thus far. But I wouldn't have traded it for anything. I did the best I could under the worst of circumstances. It's never easy to see someone you love slip away. Especially when you're the favorite.

"Let all that you do be done in love."
I Corinthians 16:14 (NRSV)

THE FINE ART OF
TELLING A JOKE

Marilynn Scherer

My father taught me everything I needed to know about telling a good joke. He was a master of timing. He had an incredible wit, and he was careful, always, to remind me that it was more important to be able to "take it" than to "dish it out". I've been blessed with the same wit and timing, which, in my earlier years, gave my father the task of teaching me the when and where of using my sense of humor.

The best example of these lessons happened on the occasion of my 11th birthday.

My 16-year-old sister, Linda, was seated at the birthday celebration dinner table, along with my mother and father. My mother had prepared my favorite meal and favorite cake (devil's food with whipped cream topping). Though I can't remember details, I can assure all readers that my sister had not spent dinner wishing me a wonderful birthday along with hopes for the coming year. She most likely kicked me under the table, complained about the dinner, and asked (frequently) if we were done and if she could be excused. She was a teenager and she was horrible.

After dinner, we had the traditional birthday cake. I was excited since presents would be soon to follow. So the candles were on my cake, and before the huffing and puffing, my mother reminded me to make a wish. I blew out the candles, and my father said, "I hope your wish comes true." I replied, "It didn't come true – Linda's still here."

Well, suffice it to say my humor was not appreciated. My mother sighed, my sister attempted to punch me, and my father chose the moment to whisk me from the dining room table and to my room for a brief conference. I thought for sure I was about to be grounded or spanked ... and on my birthday!

He closed the door. I sat on the end of my bed with my head held low. It was at that moment he burst into laughter. "That," he said, "was very funny. The problem is, you hurt your sister's feelings, and it's never okay to get a laugh at the expense of hurting someone's feelings. And, if you're going to pick on someone, pick on someone who can take it ... like me." He told me later that he fully intended to use my line.

I'm sure my sister thought I got in trouble. My mother was wise enough to ask questions much, much later. I came back to the dining room table, apologized to my sister, and continued with the celebration.

The best gift I received that day was my father's wisdom. It was the first of many times I felt the joy of making him laugh.

SHARING THE LOAD

Bob Vanlandingham

In 1953, after returning from Korea, I met a wonderful woman, Consuela Winburn. We were married on September 4, 1954. Our first child was born in 1955, and over the next 10 years we had seven more children -- a total of seven boys and one girl.

I worked hard being the "bread winner" of our large family, and Connie spent her time taking care of the kids. On weekends, she made sure that she and all the children went to Sunday School and church. I, on the other hand, spent Saturdays and Sundays golfing. It never occurred to me that Connie might have other things she would have liked to do, or that she just needed to have a break from the kids now and then. The thought simply didn't cross my mind.

One day, my father-in-law said to me, "I know you do a pretty good job of raising your family, but you need to try a little harder to help my daughter with the kids. Why don't you try trading places with her? There is more to being a father than working. You have got to help your wife, too." So, I thought about what he said and I decided my father-in-law was right.

Thus began a new chapter in our marriage. From that point on, Connie and I traded off weekends. One weekend she made plans to do what she wanted, and the next weekend I could play golf. That plan worked so well, that we stuck with it for the next 35 or 40 years. Now that our children are all grown, I think she gets more weekends than I do!

"You have a lifetime to work,
but children are only young once."
Polish Proverb

SO PROUD OF DAD

Karen Massou

Upon hearing of the childhood sexual abuse of a loved one, Jerry Hoemig constructively used his sadness and anguish to organize, expand, and bolster the work of SCAN. He volunteered as a SCAN public speaker, worked on the SCAN Financial Board, served SCAN's Board of Directors as Board President, and aided in fundraising.

So many people sit passively and turn from that which is uncomfortable, unjust, and inhuman. It takes great courage to put aside personal pain and step forward to protect, support, and illuminate. I have been honored to witness my father, Jerry Hoemig, live his life by striving to "do the right thing". He is the type of man that pours his heart and soul into remedying injustices and fighting the good fight for those who cannot fight for themselves. His work with SCAN empowered and educated people and has served to make Fort Wayne a better place to live.

<u>Pause and Reflect</u>

Take a moment and think about your own experiences with your father, your child or your grandchild.

1. What lessons did your father teach you?

2. As your mind drifts to earlier years, what is your finest memory of Dad?

3. How do you communicate the lessons you have learned from your father to your children? Do you include sights, sounds, color, and context to the stories of "Dad" to help his spirit "transcend" to the next generation?

4. As a father, stepfather or grandfather today, what memories or stories do you hope your children will recall about you?

CHAPTER 5

LIFE'S LESSONS

*"There are two lasting bequests we
can give our children. One is roots.
The other is wings."*
                                        Hodding Carter, Jr.

We teach our children, and we learn about life through use of all of our senses. Some people say the last sense to go as we age is the sense of smell. Which one of us hasn't walked into a room where something is cooking that reminds us of our childhood? Just reflect for a moment now. One can almost experience the aroma of a pot of soup, a smell of laundry detergent, or a whiff of cologne. These memories stay with us because we learn with all of our senses.

We learn from our children by watching them, listening to them, touching them. Do you recall the fear experienced with the "hot skin" of a child with fever? What parent hasn't been able to tell that the 7-year-old child who claims to have bathed but couldn't possibly have and smell the way they do. What about the smell of alcohol on the breath of a teenager that teaches us that our child needs some tempering?

Thoughts from Rachel

Life lessons are things we teach our children sometimes

just by who we are and how we handle ourselves in a given situation. I learned to handle pain and tragedy by watching my mother handle the tragic death of my uncle when I was eight. She cried in private. She got angry with my father who wrapped her in his arms and taught me that not all anger is created equal. I also learned from the millions of one-liners my mother taught me. From "wash your hands" to "we don't give up when it is hard" to "be a good soldier, don't cry". Some, of course, were good lessons – some weren't. All of these life lessons provide a foundation upon which to face life and… parenting. Here are a few.

• Parenting is like banking – be sure to be putting more in than you are taking out.

• Catch your kids being good – not just bad!

• Every parent needs to have three parenting friends. One who has younger children so you can teach them but also see how far you have come; one who has raised their children so you know you will make it; and one who has children the same age so you can commiserate with them.

• Don't threaten a discipline you can't follow through with and always follow through.

• Parenting is the hardest job you will ever have because you love them.

• The sign of a good parent is one who asks for help.

• Say yes to your teen as often as you can… it makes the no's more palatable.

• The miracle grow for children is positive words… make sure you are watering them daily.

• Parents seldom let a day go by without correcting or pointing out problems with their children… as such, don't let a day go by without telling them you love them.

• Savor every moment, the good, the worries, and the ugly. They end quickly, and when it is over it is over.

Reflections from Dave

As the father of the bride, I recently began to reflect on a few thoughts to welcome guests at the wedding of my oldest daughter, Molly, and her new husband. I told of a story that reflected on a time when Molly about age seven. I explained that with five children at that time, money was tight and vacations were never elaborate. Our summers were always filled with camping at state parks, going to an Indiana lake, visiting Cedar Point, or just picnics and bike rides. Many summers were filled with common summer fun but always included summer projects of painting, fixing, building, or remodeling. The family played and sweat together!

At the end of one summer, in one of my dad moods,
I asked the kids what they enjoyed most about the summer.
I did this expecting to hear about the roller coaster at Cedar
Point or one of our visits to the lake. I don't recall what all
my daughters said, but I do recall what Molly recited. She
looked up at me with big blue eyes and beautiful smile and
said, "Dad... do you remember when we painted the garage
together?"

I said, "yeah", slowly and guardedly...

She said, "That was fun, that was the best part of the
summer, Dad."

As I thought about Molly's words, I reflected about
the life lesson I was learning. Sometimes I get confused about
"doing for" versus "being with". I "do for" when I drive to
the soccer or football game with a child in the back seat with
headphones on. I "do for" when I cheer from the sideline at
one of their games or stop at the library to pick up a resource
for a project they might be working on. Although "doing
for" is an important part of parenting, "being with" is active
engagement. It is tossing the frisbee or football to a child, it is
biking through the park with a child on the back of a tandom,
it is teaching a child how to paint the garage and "sweating"
together as a project comes together.

Strange as it may be... sometimes our best experiences
and life lessons take place in a moment when we least expect.
Often those "best" experiences occur... when we are laughing,
crying, or just plain sweating or working together... like

painting the garage. But they occur when we get caught up in the moment with people we love and appreciate. The life lesson Molly taught me, and then I teach others, is the value of "sweat" in building and appreciating relationships.

"Life can be understood backward,
but it must be lived forward."
Soren Kierkegaard

ROOTIN' FOR THE UNDERDOG

Stephanie Jentgen

When I look back at my childhood, there are so many good memories and experiences to recount. There were picnics, vacations, holidays and parties. Even the ordinary day-in and day-out activities, such as brushing teeth, picking up toys and getting ready for bed, provided opportunities for routines that represented security and love to me and my three younger brothers.

But there is one quality that Mom and Dad fostered in me that continues to shape my destiny as an adult. They taught me that it is my responsibility to protect the "underdog", to step in when others step away.

Mom and Dad didn't lecture me about this. They didn't nag. They simply provided a living example of helping others. I still remember every time a baby bird fell out of a nest, Dad would try and save it. If there was a child being picked on at school or in the neighborhood, Mom always told me to be his or her friend so that they knew someone loved them. We always raised money for the various telethons, walkathons, and bowlathons that occurred. For parties and overnighters, we always had to invite the kids no one else would invite. And we were not allowed to pass out Valentines or cookies unless EVERYONE would receive one.

There were opportunities within my own family to practice this acceptance as well. My Dad's sister was mentally retarded (the term at that time); she functioned at about a third grade level. Rather than letting her languish alone in a state school, we regularly visited her and brought her home to stay with us one to two weeks at a time a few times each year. The whole family would drive up to the state school, run up to her cottage and wait expectantly for Aunt Bertie to come join us.

She was so much fun! She loved Pepsi, the Detroit Tigers and loudly singing Christmas carols off-key. We would play games with her and ask her to tell us about her "boyfriend," Ricky. We weren't frightened of her or embarrassed by her. In fact, I would become fiercely and vocally protective of her when other kids, and even adults, would stare rudely or make snide remarks. I learned to love and respect all people. And I learned how cruel the rest of the world could be to those who appeared different.

Looking back, I can see that I always felt compassion and concern for the "underdogs" in my life. My favorite cartoon characters include Charlie Brown and Ziggy. And I rarely missed an episode of <u>Underdog</u> when it was on. Heck, I still smile when I remember Shoeshine Boy emerging from the telephone booth as Underdog saying, "When Polly's in trouble, I am not slow, it's up, up, up and away I go!"

Today, I continue to root for the underdog. My professional life, volunteer life, and a good part of my personal life is dedicated to helping God's creatures that seem to have been abandoned by others. It's not even something I have planned. It just worked out this way. This has helped me remain grateful for all that I have, and, to be honest, all that I don't have. And it all started with Mom and Dad's gentle souls and generous hearts.

"To bring up a child in the way he should go, travel that way yourself."

Josh Billings

ADOLESCENT ADVENTURE

Amy Knepp

It was a Friday afternoon and I was taking some time
out just to relax (yes, RELAX!) when in waltzed my 18-year-
old son with a Cheshire cat grin on his face. My first words
were, "What did you do?" Sheepishly he proceeded to tell
me that he had received a 1½ hour after-school community
service discipline (which would not be completed until the
following Friday) for acts that were both humorous and
outrageous to say the least.

You have to know my son. He is one of the most
modest, quiet, responsible young men that I know. His
willingness to explore new things and take risks is one of his
characteristics I admire the most. He's so different from me!
When I was a teenager, I never would step out and risk being
noticed. I hated to draw attention to myself. Austin, on the
other hand, isn't afraid to know and be known.

On that Friday afternoon, the weather had turned
bad, and a torrential thunderstorm had indeed soaked our
already soggy land with more rain. Some buddies of Austin's
dared him to run outside during the rain in his boxer shorts.
Now, he doesn't just wear boxers beneath his clothing. The
boxers are indeed the teen "attire" of the times. Guys just
wear them under everything (or so it seems). So he was clad
in briefs, boxers, then his shorts, t-shirt, shoes and socks.
Being a pragmatist, he took off his shoes and socks to prevent

them from getting wet. Next, he removed his outer shorts
and t-shirt. Off he went into the rain, running in front of
the school room window so his classmates would be sure to
know of his "daring" success. Obviously this violated some
behavior expectations of the high school, and needless to say,
he was caught in the act and disciplined. Both my husband and
I thought it a fair and just punishment for his risk of the day.
Life went on.

     Have you ever been busy at something and received the
unexpected? Five days following Austin's rain-jogging event, I
received a phone call from the high school informing me that
they were changing his discipline to a three-day suspension
rather than the 1½ hour after-school community service.
As a parent, this raised some concern. It wasn't the original
discipline for the act that was being questioned; it had seemed
fair and appropriate. What I questioned was the decision of
the school administration to change the discipline five days
after the fact. What message does this send to adolescents?
Does this mean that in the workplace they never can be sure
of what will happen after mistakes are made? Does this mean
that punishment, in whatever form, can be reconsidered and
reinvented? Consistency in how parents discipline is key to
children learning responsibility and respect for authority.
The school's action brought confusion and emotions to an
inexperienced, unsuspecting adolescent who thought all was
settled. Trust was broken and respect shaken.

     As life moves forward for all of us, we hope to take the

experiences we have and learn - even grow - from them. Here
are the lessons learned. First, life isn't fair. This was a good
lesson for Austin to learn. Sometimes as parents we try so
hard to be fair and just, but life just isn't.

Second, consistency in discipline promotes respect
and trust. Without trust and respect, greater gaps develop
between kids and adults. Once broken, mending trust is not
done quickly. It requires time and effort.

Third, respect of authority must be demonstrated,
even if the decisions are wrong. Austin saw us discuss the
situation with the school administrators and, in the end,
appropriately respect their decision. We didn't have to agree
with their decision to show respect.

Fourth, while risk-taking is admirable and in some
situations even desirable, you must choose carefully which
risks you take. To step out and take a risk can be a huge event
(or even an accomplishment, depending on the action) for an
adolescent. As parents we must be careful not to squelch the
spirit within our child for a momentary poor decision. It is our
desire to continue to nurture that adventurous spirit without
destroying his individuality.

And finally, we as parents must advocate for our
children. If we don't, who will? Adolescents are not adults
and we cannot expect them to make decisions as an adult.
Developmentally they just aren't there yet. It is a learning
process, it seems, not only for the children, but for adults and
institutions as well.

LEARNING INDEPENDENCE

Michael A. Lewandowski

My parents were always very determined to instill independence in their children. They always offered me encouragement, suggestions, and support, but they were adamant that I learn to do things for myself. Those things included school projects, paper routes, repairing my bicycle, finishing jobs on the "job list", and making decisions for just about everything. As a child, I always found this annoying. I would ask, "Why can't you just do this for me rather than making me do it?" Now that I'm an adult, I look back on those experiences and realize how much they influenced my life. Independence became one of my most valued traits, and I worked hard to instill it in my own children. It still amazes me how much something that I hated as a child became one of those things for which I'm most grateful as an adult.

A WINNING ARGUMENT

Eleanor H. Marine

My youngest daughter was in the sixth grade when we had a knock down, drag out argument one morning before she left for school. Later that morning, on the way to school, her father told her that she was never to argue with me again.

Obviously this bothered her, because the following day when she returned from school, she mustered all of her courage and stood in front of me. She politely informed me that her father had told her to never argue with me. Then she simply looked at me and waited for a reply.

I smiled inside and told her that I knew what her father had said, but I expected her to continue to argue with me. In her frustration she began to cry and said, "But, I can't ever win."

"Keep trying," I replied. "You will one of these days." Happily, she did continue to argue with me, and, expectedly, she did begin to win.

MONEY MATTERS

Jerri Lerch

Over the years, we've met other parents who have
children a few years older than ours, and we've learned a great
deal from them. We've also helped other parents who have
children a few years younger than our own. We are not the
originators of many of the good techniques that we've used;
we've borrowed them and enhanced them, as others have
done.

Despite having a reasonably comfortable family
income, we've tried from the beginning to avoid becoming
materialistic. It's natural that children, as well as many adults,
want all the goods and toys that they can comfortably get. But
we didn't want that to be our children's focus. To put off the
dreaded day when our children became brand conscious, we
helped them create a budget.

For years we gave our children a small allowance of
$2 a week, plus special holiday gifts from others. This
allowance wasn't payment for routine chores around the
house. We felt household chores are part of the family
obligation that we all share, regardless of pay. Rather, an
allowance is to teach children about money management. A
budget is about money management as well.

When our children were in middle school, we asked
them to estimate their regular expenses including school
lunches, clothes, shoes, haircuts, music, electronics, personal

hygiene items, birthday party gifts for others, and routine recreation. We agreed to cover items such as school activity fees, sporting expenses, and summer camp fees. We did not want them to economize themselves out of activities supporting their own good development. If they needed new athletic shoes, we would cover the average price of a pair of shoes in the marketplace. If they wanted premium brands or styles, they would be responsible for paying the difference. We paid for dance and music lessons. Any time that they did not feel like going to a lesson that we had paid for, they would owe us $10 as a repayment, no questions asked. Whenever our children could justify that their expenses had legitimately increased, we were happy to adjust their budgets. We only adjusted our younger child's once, by $20 per month, as she entered high school.

We gave our children their allowance, by check, once a month. To receive their check, each child had to submit an accounting of how they spent or saved their money the month before. We were rarely critical of their purchases. Just tracking money spent on a regular basis was a good educational experience for all of us. This review of expenses needed to be done by the fifth of the month. If they were late, they lost $10 per day of their new payment. Once in a while they missed a month, and eventually, missed the money.

When our son and daughter began driving, we provided them with transportation as long as they were getting good grades and were active in extra-curricular activities. We wanted school and leadership success to be their primary job. Later, we asked them to pay for their own gas, get receipts, and we reimbursed them for half of their gas expense. They both opted to have at least one, if not two, part-time jobs throughout high school and college.

Our children decided when they needed new jeans or designer shoes. The very first month of his new budget, we skeptically watched our son decide to buy some very expensive athletic shoes in a large department store in a large city. He wore those shoes for the next four years before he bought new ones. After years of keeping their extra money in shoe boxes and putting accumulations of cash into money market accounts, they arrived, in high school, to manage their own checkbooks and debit accounts. When our daughter was in high school, she became the Student Council treasurer, and later Student Council President of a very large high school, due to her budgeting skills. When our son was 18 and preparing to begin college, my husband sent him to independently meet with our financial advisor. He came home and told us that he felt a Roth IRA (a retirement planning tool) would be the best long-term investment for himself with at least some of his funds. In college, we suggested that our son seek a credit card account. There are so many offers of credit cards on college campuses, waiting to take advantage of students' impulse buys and poor payment patterns. He refused our suggestion as he didn't think it was personally necessary.

Teaching our children financial responsibility and how to use financial instruments is a key part of our responsibility as parents. I feel that we do them a disservice to let them believe that there are limitless resources or to deny them the opportunity to prioritize their resources within their own lives.

"Give a man a fish and you feed him for a day. Teach a man to fish and you feed him for a lifetime."
Chinese Proverb

A TRIBUTE TO MY GRANDMA

Catherine J. Fruchey

My grandmother died at 98-1/2 years of age. At her funeral, often through tears and channeling the voice and feelings of a six-year-old little girl (in my 53-year-old body), I shared the following remarks with friends and family.

A Tribute To My Grandma

Bernice Adeline Stookey

July 19, 1905–April 12, 2004

Today as we say goodbye to Grandma and celebrate her life, I'd like to say a few words in honor of Grandma and what she brought to my life.

When I was a child I often felt awkward and unlovable, but not with Grandma. She made me feel special, and she did it in these seemingly simple ways:

- Grandma always was happy to see me. Whether it was with words or a warm smile, she let me know she enjoyed my visits. She enjoyed me. I felt important.

- She spent time with me, listened to me, and talked to me like I was her equal, a desirable companion, not just a child. I felt valued.

- Grandma had a remarkable memory and often regaled

us with stories of her younger days. My children, Shannon and Michael, always loved that about her, and called her tales "stories of the olden days". Her eagerness to share her life and roots with me, and later with my children, made me feel connected and grounded.

One of my favorite memories of Grandma is a visual image of myself, around grade-school age, sitting on the cool gray cement steps of her back porch. From my perch, I watched Grandma, in her print cotton housedress, hoe in hand, going after the pesky weeds that invaded her flowerbeds. I could see she derived much pleasure from the earth and working outside in her garden. I'd ask all kinds of questions and Grandma would take time to answer them all, patiently and kindly.

These deceptively simple acts, yet truly amazing things she did, showed me she loved me. Grandma's interactions with me had a magical power that transformed my view of myself. The way in which she demonstrated her love for me gave me the building blocks to love myself and to become the woman I am today.

Grandma nurtured me as naturally and as lovingly as she tended her garden. She didn't learn how to garden or how to love people from a book or a class – these talents came naturally to her. She instinctively knew how to nourish me, to give me the things I hungered for – to be seen, to be heard, and to be loved unconditionally.

Because of Grandma's wondrous gift of knowing how to love well, our family blossomed under her care. I know I did. I would not be who I am today if I had not been blessed by my Grandma's love.

Thank you, Grandma.

I love you.

"I remember my mother's prayers and they have always followed me. They have clung to me all my life."

Abraham Lincoln

SHADOW IN THE CORNER

Patty E. Barrand

In the daylight, you look around and
you see a shadow in the corner

Only one person knows where the shadow is

It waits for the silence and night
to be able to escape its problems
It cries silently in its corner to try to forget
the beating it just received

When out of its corner, it covers its
bruises as much as possible

There's an open door ahead,
but the shadow can't move

It finally sees two trusting arms
reaching out to it

When out of its corner, the shadow sees
a beautiful angel with wings spread out
to protect it

This shadow in the corner,

that only felt

fear,

is that of a lost, little angel with broken wings

With guidance and support from its

guardian angel,

it becomes a beautiful

angel itself, not a shadow in the corner.

"Waste not fresh tears over old griefs."

Euripides

Jammie Races

Jerri Lerch

When our children were young and we wanted to expedite bed-time preparations, we'd have "jammie races". We would be in the car, traveling home from an evening activity, and either my husband or myself would announce that we were going to have a "jammie race" when we got home. There were no prizes other than bragging rights, but the garage door would go up, the car would go to "park", seat belts would be flying, and the kids would be running through the kitchen and hallway, pulling off their clothes as they ran. My husband would sometimes pull on their shirts or pants, slowing them down, resulting in short-lived wailing. We had fun.

We had so much fun that not until last year, at the ripe age of 18, our daughter suddenly recognized that the jammie races were an adult ploy to put the children to bed more quickly. She immediately wanted to know what other useful "tricks" we as parents had played on her and her brother. In fact, she plans on having her own "jammie races" some day in the distant future when she has her own children. The fun continues....

BLENDED FAMILIES
ACROSS GENERATIONS

Nancy Nightingale Gillespie

My mother's grandmother raised her because she
was born when her mother was only 16 years old. No one
in the family knew she was pregnant until she doubled over
and screamed during her bath in the tub in the kitchen. Her
sister yelled, "Ma! Ma! Come quick, Mart's having a baby." My
mother's father had already abandoned the family. When he
returned with an offer of marriage 17 years later, neither my
mother nor grandmother took him seriously.

My mother's childhood consisted of being sent back
and forth between her mother and grandmother, depending
on who had enough to feed her. In school, the kids teased her
because she had no father. Some of her mother's boyfriends
were nice, others were not. She learned survival skills at an
early age and grew up cynical and wary.

My mother met my father when she was 22. He was
a decade older than her and was raising two children, ages
10 and 11, from a previous marriage. This was something my
mother had never experienced, a man who hadn't run away,
a man who stayed and raised the children. They were soon
married and settled in to raise nine more children together.

I have five sisters and five brothers. I was my father's
fifth child and my mother's third. Six children followed me,
completing our family of 11. I didn't realize that my oldest

brother and sister actually were my stepbrother and sister until
I was six years old. I was in first grade and we were drawing
our family trees, literally drawing trees and writing family
names on the branches. What kind of branches do you draw
for stepchildren? I went home and asked.

My mother was quick to respond, "You draw the same
branches for Mary and Rolland as for your other brothers
and sisters." I completed my family tree and showed it to my
family. My mother said, "It's no one's business which child
came from where. We're all family here." And we were.

Because my stepsister was so much older than me,
when I was five, I was the flower girl in her wedding. My
sisters and I fought over whose turn it was to sleep overnight
at her house. And when she had children, we argued over who
was going to babysit. When my 19-year-old stepbrother was
on leave from the Marines, he died in a car accident. He and
his friend skidded on ice and flew over the side of the bridge.
We all cried. We were family and nothing was more important
than family.

In June of 1967, I was an innocent 17-year-old. It was
the summer before my senior year and I was busy reading
books, going swimming, and growing up. I met a man who was
23 and fell in love. Two months later, I was pregnant and my
boyfriend abandoned me. One night, I was at an engagement
party with my closest girlfriend. She had left with another
person and I realized it was past curfew. I knew my mother
would be very angry, so when one of the guys said, "I'll drive

anyone home who needs a ride", I got into his car with seven other teens and young adults. He took a corner too fast and we were involved in a horrible car accident.

The girl who had become engaged that night died. I fractured most of the bones on my left side, and almost died from internal bleeding. My mother was not about to lose another child; she sat and prayed by my bed for days. Three days after the car accident, the doctor informed me that I had suffered so much internal damage the baby would be born dead or severely handicapped. During my three-month hospitalization, surgeons placed two steel rods along my backbone to stabilize it. I was paralyzed and lay on a striker frame, a bed that looks like a cot. The nurses would put another similar cot on top, secure the straps on each side, and turn me from my back to my stomach, and later, to my back again. When my back healed, I was able to stand and walk with the aid of crutches. I went home to a hospital bed in the living room. I stayed there for six weeks until I learned to crutch up and down the steps to my bedroom. I was able to walk without the crutches one week before I went to deliver my son.

The moment I saw my newborn son, my life changed. I looked into his eyes and he looked into mine. We were family and nothing is more important than family. Then I counted fingers and toes and checked his small, perfect body. I loved him before he was born, but I had imagined all kinds of horrible things that could be wrong with him during the hours I lay paralyzed in the hospital and during the hours I lay in the hospital bed in my parents' living room. I was so relieved, all I could do was hold him and love him and cry.

My son and I married a man later that year. Together we had two more sons and then four years of family evaporated into divorce. I was alone with my sons. My mother and father had survived against the odds; they were still together. I was not so lucky. I became a divorce statistic. My children became single-parent children, again.

I was 22 years old and my husband had run off with our teenage babysitter. I had obtained my GED during my second pregnancy and my driver's license just before my third child was born. Vocational Rehabilitation helped me go to college. Finances were tight, but I knew if we survived, I could keep my family together. I was in my second year of college when I met Bob. Bob and I, along with my sons, started dating and since Bob is from a blended family, he knows how important family is.

He and I blended our family and this year celebrated 32 years of togetherness. It seems like only yesterday that my mother told me the story of her mother, in the tub, in the kitchen. I'll remember to tell my children the story, over and over, so it doesn't get lost. Blended families are "family" – the most important thing of all.

SILENT CRY

Patty E. Barrand

You wake up to start another day in
fear of what you will do wrong that day.
As a child, you don't understand why
you can't do it right
You wait for the next blow that
leaves a mark that takes away a piece
of your heart.
At night you lay in bed in the dark
and pray for someone
to hear your silent cry.
No one sees it, or hears it,
but it's there.
It's a cry of fear and felt
deep inside.
One day someone does recognize that
silent cry, and helps your world become
one of love…
But that silent cry is never forgotten.

STARTING THEM YOUNG

Jerri Lerch

Today, I went to parent orientation for freshmen students at the university. Our baby girl is going away to college. We were asked, as parents, what our greatest fears for our children are as they start the college experience. Many parents in the group quickly talked about basic skills, such as finishing homework, getting up in the morning on a timely basis, and time management skills. Thankfully, my worries are few and I do not share those concerns.

Our children were four or five years old when I gave them each an alarm clock for their bedrooms. I bought a cute little cube with pink and turquoise buttons for our daughter, which she still uses today. I helped them set the alarms, showed them how to play the music and how to turn the clocks off. They thought it was a big deal and couldn't wait to begin using their grown-up clocks. Our daughter knew all of the song lyrics to the "oldies" as she would spend hours in her bedroom, writing on her chalkboard, playing with her toys, and listening to her radio.

To ease them into using their new clocks, we designated some "special" days as alarm clock days, and some days as regular days. On alarm clock days, the children were responsible for setting their clocks and getting up on time. Each of our two children was late for middle school not more than twice in their academic lives, and never were they tardy for work. Our son was on the swimming team for a year or two in middle school, and came to our bedroom, dressed and ready to go at 4:30 am on designated swim practice mornings. Frequently he had to make sure we, his parents, were up and ready to go!

Similarly, we started our son and daughter on household tasks when they still thought it was a big deal to "get to" do something. We pulled chairs up to the kitchen sink for them to stand on and help with dishes.

We even taught our children to take care of their own laundry at an early age. This came in handy, especially since our son had enuresis, or night time bed-wetting, into his elementary school years. This was not a source of shame for him, nor did we punish him for his accidents. Instead, we taught him to operate the washer and dryer at an early age. He was small for his age and had to use a chair to climb up to twist the knobs, but he was proud that he could take care of it himself. No one else had to be involved in his personal matters. We were, of course, aware, but we did not interfere. Our neighbors, with children slightly older than ours, suggested that children do their own laundry at the age of ten or twelve. Our children, as teen-agers, thought it was an intrusion if we did their personal laundry.

Because we helped our children become independent and resourceful at a young age, they now enjoy great self-confidence. I believe it's the chief task of any parent to bring their children into independent functioning for adulthood, to give them the confidence and permission to succeed. It's part of giving children roots and wings.

As our daughter begins her college experience 1,600 miles away from home, I am not worried for her. She's had lots of successful practice. Besides, the little cube alarm clock with the cute pink and turquoise buttons is right by her side.

"Children have more need of models than critics."
French Proverb

UNWANTED TOUCH

Patty E. Barrand

Being a child in this world today, you
put your trust in a lot of people.
Then you find out, there are people
that take that trust and use it against you.

They do the most distrustful thing
anyone can do to a person.
It's the unwanted touch.

You're left alone with a friend.
They take away one thing you have for them
and that is trust.
They did it with the unwanted touch.

It's a touch you won't forget in a lifetime.
And every time it happens you can't say anything
'cause of the threat to your family.

This friend becomes your enemy with
his unwanted touch.

In the years to come, you try to forget
what had happened in the past,
but you never forget
that unwanted touch.

A LIFE OF ADVENTURE

Adrienne M. Clark

I once found myself with a friend having one of those introspective conversations about why we make the decisions we make. She and I had gone shopping in her station wagon because mine wasn't running at the time. We had just unloaded groceries for me and my six children and were resting on the station wagon tail gate. Since we were talking about past decisions and their consequences, the subject of my ex-husband came up, of course.

"Why did you marry him?" she asked.

I thought a bit and replied, "Because I was looking for adventure and he was my ticket to an adventurous life." I paused a moment and added, "I guess I got what I asked for. I just never imagined my adventure was going to be raising six kids, by myself, in a small town in Indiana."

The two of us lay back in the station wagon and laughed until the kids were looking at us like we were crazy.

That conversation helped me to see parenting in a new light. It really is an adventure... a very long and exciting adventure, with new twists and turns at every step in the road. We are always wondering if we are doing the right thing, or saying the right thing. We are always worried about what is around the next corner.

Nothing much about parenting is carved in stone and what works for one child or in one family won't work in another. The advice of one expert may be best for your family, but the advice of another expert may be better for mine.

It made my life a lot easier to remember that part of the adventure of parenting is experimenting – never knowing for sure what is going to work and what isn't. Being right isn't nearly as important as trying… and being willing to admit when it isn't working.

Parenting is one life-long experiment. If one thing doesn't work, try another. If one plan goes awry, make a new one. It's just one grand, long-term adventure! We can either fight it or struggle through it feeling really bad when we aren't "right", or we can enjoy the adventure of the grand experiment. It's really up to us.

BROKEN PIECES

Patty E. Barrand

As I stand looking in the mirror
I am a grown woman
All I see is broken pieces

These broken pieces are of the past
Each piece I see myself as a child
A child scared, bruised and silent
A child not knowing whom to reach out to
Who she can trust

As I look deeper into some pieces they become clear
These are pieces of the present
Ones of which I have learned to trust and love

When these pieces are put together
They show you can put the betrayal
And hurt of the past in one piece and
Live for a future of LOVE

A FAMILY OF MY OWN

Tammy Van Baalen

I didn't come from mommy's tummy,

I don't have daddy's chin.

But, I am theirs just the same and that's how this begins.

Mommy and Daddy told me a story

about how I was born.

It was filled with special words

and pictures that were worn.

They held me tight and kissed me lots

and even once I saw them cry.

But, they said they were tears of happiness

just thinking 'bout the day I arrived.

They shared how much they wanted me

and how they had to wait.

And when the time had come to meet me

they would never forget the date.

They talked about my "birth" mommy

and how she loved me so.

That she was brave and caring

protecting me till our first hello.

They spoke so soft and took great care.

They wanted me to understand.

And… I could feel they loved me

as they tightly squeezed my hands.

I know they worried 'bout how I'd feel

Would I believe their goodness and trust that they were real?

But it was now my turn to tell them

what I had come to know.

That the family who loves and cares for me is a

family all my own.

And yes, now I know the story about

how I came to be with my mom and dad.

That we were always meant to be a family;

the best any kid could ever hope to have.

PAUSE AND REFLECT

Take a moment and think about your own experiences with your parents, your child or your grandchild.

1. Close your eyes and think about the sights, sounds, smells, and touch of your parents, children or grandchildren. What are the first thoughts that come to your mind?

2. What are the "one-liners" you've heard from your parents or others about parenting?

3. What "life lessons" do you tell other parents with children younger than yours?

4. As you reflect on the journey of learning from one generation, and passing wisdom onto the next, what stories do you recall that capture the essence of these lessons?

CHAPTER 6

WHEN ALL IS SAID AND DONE

If I can stop one heart from breaking,
I shall not live in vain;
Or cool one pain,
Or help one fainting robin
Unto his nest again,
I shall not live in vain.

Emily Dickinson

Memories and stories of our lives come in all variations. They are short, long, joy-filled, reflective, funny, and sad. They contain truths, or at least our version of reality. They are often about lessons learned in the journey of life. Memories are created through use of all of our senses. Some of the memories are told as stories verbally or in writing. Memories told as stories often pass on a richness of tradition and a legacy of our lives.

Thoughts from Rachel

I can remember the smell of my mother's handkerchiefs she would loan me in church long after I was grown up because I never had a Kleenex. I can still feel the warmth of my father's kiss on my cheek and how he felt when I hugged his head. There is nothing like the site of my hometown area to bring a flood of emotions, nostalgia and stories.

People share their stories with each other all the time. In the past month I have heard a wonderful Christmas story from a man who wanted a Lionel train for Christmas and got it. I have heard a daughter tell a warm memory of playing with her dad as a child. I have heard another story of pain and recovery from a woman whose parents divorced when she was a teen. She shares her story with other parents who are divorcing in hopes it will leave them with some thoughts and considerations as they move forward. These stories reveal inner truths and perspectives on life.

In my collection of mementos are two letters my father wrote in the last year before he died. These letters represent a piece of him, his thoughts, his feelings, and tell part of his story. Aside from these letters, the only thing that I have that confirms his existence is the stories he created while alive. I retell these stories to my children often. They are a rich tradition in our family.

Reflections from Dave

As a nurse and therapist, I often hear stories of pain and grief that accompany life's journey. In sharing "out loud" verbally or in writing, one helps to clarify that which is held in head and heart. Pausing and reflecting creates a healing space for individuals who have emotional bruises and scars.

The process of making that which is inside the head and heart a "multi-sensory" experience need not only be reserved for those with emotional pain. The telling of story and the writing of memories helps to create a sense of permanence, purpose, and legacy from one generation to the next. As parents, the pause and reflect of who we are and how we parent creates intentionality in our parenting style. It suggests the high importance of this life role.

I seek opportunities and love to hear the stories from my children about their "perception" of what happened during their childhood. Elizabeth and Rachael often recall a vivid story about one afternoon in their early childhood. They talk about "the day" our car broke down and we played a mysterious game at Lawton Park while we waited for the car to be fixed. Jenny tells of a hide-and-go-seek game where I turned out the lights and scared the bejeebers out of her and her sisters. On Christmas we re-read the notes that the kids wrote to Santa and the "hidden" messages that Santa wrote back to help "guide them" through the next year. The stories sometimes get embellished, but laying close to the surface is the precious value of connecting heart with spirit. Treasure the stories! They allow us to share the riches of our lives.

PAUSE AND REFLECT

Each of us has a story, a memory, or reflection from our past. It most likely began with our parents. Creating happy stories has been a large part of the work we do at SCAN. Our job is to help parents create happy tomorrows and memories for children; to make sure the legacy they leave are like the stories in this book.

The closing pages of this book are empty. They are waiting for you to fill them with your memories and stories of parenting or being parented. When we first began this book many people were hesitant to include their memories and stories because they said, "I can't write." The style of writing is not what is important; it is in the pause and reflection of memories where one captures the essence and purpose of life's memories. When it is all said and done, what we leave behind are these stories, these moments of joy, fun, happiness, lessons, and memories.

We encourage you to make sharing of your stories a tradition. Write some of them down on these pages. Keep the memories alive. If you have not done so already:

- Start a tradition of telling stories at family gatherings.
- Have a time after Thanksgiving or holiday dinner where you share stories of the past.
- Make weddings a time to reflect and share stories of the couple.

- Write a short memory or story in a birthday card.
- On children's birthday, retell the story of the day they were born.
- When the lights are out at bedtime, whisper the story of how important your child has been to you today and always.
- Know that spontaneous moments are often the best stories and should be remembered.
- Leave behind the stories and morals you want to live on through your sharing.
- As parents age, sit with them and record their life lessons that the desire you to pass on to the next generation.
- When all is said and done, it is these stories that will live on and enrich the world.